STORIES
FOR MY
GRANDCHILDREN

Sandra Rider
1125 11th St
Bloomington, IL 61704

STORIES FOR MY GRANDCHILDREN

Charles F. McCannon, DVM

E-BookTime, LLC
Montgomery, Alabama

Stories For My Grandchildren

Copyright © 2005 by Carolyn McCannon Peterson

All rights reserved. No part of this book may be reproduced or transmitted in any form or by any means, electronic or mechanical, including photocopying, recording, or by any information storage and retrieval system, without permission in writing from the copyright owner.

Library of Congress Control Number: 2005932518

ISBN: 1-59824-064-1

First Edition
Published August 2005
E-BookTime, LLC
6598 Pumpkin Road
Montgomery, AL 36108
www.e-booktime.com

Endorsements From the Grandchildren

"He's like me but without the annoying Yorkshire accent." ———James Herriot

"A Good egg." ———P.G. Wodehouse

"Maple Avenue is like Yoknanpatawpha County except a lot easier to pronounce." ———William Faulkner

But seriously...
"Some friends of mine, who prefer something more personal than green bean casserole from their guests, invited me to their house for Thanksgiving last year. They asked that each guest bring something personal to share. I brought along a copy of my grandfather's memoirs and read them stories. They were greeted with much laughter and applause and now tales of Mooreville and McLean County are well-known to people who have never been east of Burbank, California. Rereading these twice, thrice, fourfold-told tales again is like going back in time, not only to my grandfather's childhood but to my own when I heard them the first time. And that's a great gift to have." ———Ted Peterson

"I remember hearing and enjoying these stories so much - with this printed edition of Grandfather's memoirs, I'll always be able to hear these stories again, and when my daughter May is older she can read them, too."
———Samuel Barasch

"No matter what happened- whether I wrecked my parent's car, quit the football team or went skydiving for my thirtieth birthday - my grandfather has always had a story for every occasion, giving me hope and comfort in my own journey. Rereading these tales of a life well-lived and well-told, I find myself awed, inspired and grinning ear to ear." ————Michael Peterson

"Anecdotes amuse, entertain and inform in every letter I've received from Grandfather McCannon. At last the stories are compiled in a tome which shall make a fine addition to any library and a beloved addition to my own." ————Sarah Barasch

Contents

Forward 9
Introduction 11
Early Years 13
    Mooreville 21
    The Bullies of the Seventh Grade 29
    Skunk Hunting 35
    The Rinkydinks 39
    The Horses on the Farm 46
    The Crime Wave on Maple Avenue 51
    The Haunted House 56
    High School Daze 59
    The Great Depression 69
Illinois State Normal University 85
Iowa City and George L. Stanton 91
George and the Gold-Plated Dresser Set 99
The U.S. Weather Bureau 103
University of Iowa Summer School 111
Arabella 116
The Civil Aeronautics Administration 121
Cassoday, Kansas 126
Chanute, Kansas 130
Veterinary School 133
The Large Animal (Farm) Practice 140
    The Detective 143
    Caesarian Sections 148
    Thornton Thorpe's Stallion 152
    Smokey 155
    The Towanderosa 164
    Right Name – Wrong Cow 169
    Tympany, Hypocalcaemia and Prolapse 174

Contents

Dog Psychology 181
Duke 184
Eliza 187
Fritzel 191
Corky 193
Baird's Dalmatian 195
The Biting Peke 196
The Saint Bernards 198
Other Canine Acquaintances 202
The Horned Animal 205
Euthanasia 210
Golf 215
Carolyn and Paul O'Brien 219
Harry Schockey 222
On Leaving Private Practice 226
   Animal Control 229
   Other Animal Complaints 238
Aftermath 242
Birthday Letter: August 1990 243
Lioness Episode 247
Panic Stricken Deer Dies after Spree in IWU
Building 250
Appendices 253
   Written in a letter to the Petersons on
   May 26, 2005 253
   McCannon Family Tree 256
   Index 257
Acknowledgements 265

Forward

My family likes to tell stories, usually about ourselves and usually at least partially true. On many occasions-birthdays, successes, illnesses/injuries, my dad would write up a story on his old portable Corona (until recently the one I took to college) and mail it off to a family member. When I was growing up, his stories to me often began "When I was a little girl..."

I remember Dad's stories as being humorous; after all, didn't he read us *Cheaper by the Dozen* every summer for at least five years in a row? He next introduced my sister and me to all the P.G. Wodehouse stories by reading out loud and chuckling over the adventures of Bertie and Jeeves.

Dad never refused our requests to retell a favorite story. He would relax a bit, get a twinkle in his bright blue eyes and begin a yarn of adventure. His stories were always upbeat, sometimes they held a subtle moral but usually they were remembrances of happy times. Family struggles were told in a lighthearted way; for example, "We didn't suffer in The Depression. Everyone on Maple Avenue lived just like we did. I had the same food and the same clothes as Willard Wilson or the Longbreaks."

Dad does not want to think of his life as remarkable but he rode a horse to high school and after college earned his private pilot's license. He walked two miles to Illinois State Normal School as it was called then where his sister Minnie paid his fees but twelve years later went

Forward

for five more years of veterinary school with two daughters and a wife. He could recite poetry on long rides, give my sister Nancy math riddles to solve as we traveled to Kansas State basketball games and predict weather.

For years after we were married, my husband Charles call my father "The Prince". He seemed to do everything well. There are no stories in this volume about his bridge or pool playing abilities – which are excellent. But if pressed, Dad will admit he had no swimming skills but could dive and once he was in the water, walk quickly to the side of the pool. Dad would not want to be called The Prince since he regularly reminded us of the pitfalls of Pride.

As I was preparing this book, without his knowledge, I reminded Dad of my meeting Wilt Chamberlain and telling him I had seen him play against Kansas State. Dad quickly said, "I think you were remembering Clyde Lovellette, KU's star center from Philadelphia that every coach wanted. The only team to beat Kansas University when Lovellette played there was K-State whose team consisted of Lou Hitch, Jack Stone, and Ed Head. Tomorrow I will remember the rest of that team, but not today. Chamberlain didn't play for KU until 1955 and we left Kansas in 1953."

So this book isn't for my father who doesn't need reminding but for our family and friends. Dad wrote these stories with love and it is with love and respect that I have them published. **Happy 90th Birthday, Dad.**

Love and laughter!
Carolyn McCannon Peterson
September 19, 2005

Introduction

By Charles F. McCannon, DVM

For one to indulge in the whim of writing his own life story, it is usually inferred that he amounted to something somewhere along the line of his life, had accumulated a store of wealth, made some great discovery, or at least had some sensational notoriety of interest along the line of bank robbing, petty grafting, bigamy or other lurid escapades.

In all these interesting pursuits, I would have to plead innocent. I never created much of anything, made any great discoveries and certainly life's golden hoard has avoided me like a hypochondriac shying away from the Bubonic Plague. Neither has the long arm of the law or the mores of Society held any serious reservations as to the propriety of accepting me as a citizen. A hostess once viewed me as suspect when, during a high school party, someone got into the dessert ahead of time; but in this I was innocent. I doubt if the Thorpes accepted my innocent plea, but weeks later I found that my cousin Roy Rolofson and Kelly Bishop, who weren't invited, were the culprits.

Yes, this is an abridged autobiography. But why should biographies be restricted to only the rich, the famous or the notorious? Of course we have a wealth of history and biography available – but surprisingly little

Introduction

of real personal nature. Late in life we begrudge the oversight of not having questioned our parents, grandparents and great grandparents about their early life.

When my mother and her mother were elderly, they did recount many stories of their youth, but from my dad or my grandfathers – hardly any reminiscences at all. My grandfather McCannon in 1877 drove a team and a covered wagon across Iowa, leading a Jersey cow to homestead in Nebraska. After two years of being starved out by drought, he drove back, leading the same Jersey, from Nebraska across Iowa to DeWitt Country, Illinois – never to leave there again. I didn't know that until more than thirty years after he died when it was casually mentioned by one of my elderly aunts.

Neither was I, or for that matter, my parents aware that my great grandfather, Spencer Turner, was successfully defended in a manslaughter case by a certain Abraham Lincoln and Stephen A. Douglas. This was casually learned one hundred years after the event. This was the only time that Lincoln and Douglas were on the same side in any controversy. It was only in recent years that we found our relationship to Ann Rutledge of New Salem and Lincoln lore.

So the reason for all these reminiscences is obvious – For Ted, Samuel, Michael and Sarah, all who have at various times clamored to hear of the old days – this is what life was like from 1920 to the 1980's.

Early Years

George Stanton, whose name will be found frequently among these pages, used to reminisce about many characters he knew. One was an elderly character who, when taking in a few shots of alcohol, would go into a routine of recounting his life story. He always started out, "At the early age of nothin' I was born..."

So here goes – At the early age of nothing, I was born! This event was on September 19, 1915 (hearsay evidence – I have no memory of the event) at Wapella, Illinois in a house belonging to my Grandmother McCannon. She was a Turner – the daughter of Spencer Turner – and the house represented all she salvaged from his estate. He had some property but many children so my grandmother didn't fare too well as an heir. My parents lived in this house some four or five years. Dad farmed eighty acres north of town and did other jobs that required a team of horses. He used his team and slip (like a small bulldozer) in helping to lay the old roadbed-Highway 2 – that would bisect the state and later become one of the first paved highways of Illinois. He also used his team to haul freight to and from the Illinois Central freight yards and carried passengers needing

Early Years

transportation from the depot. He even helped unload circus wagons and pulled some wagons in nearby towns during the circus season. That was how he got his nickname. It seems there was a newspaper cartoon character – sort of a Tom Sawyer type – who ran away from home and joined the circus. The cartoon no longer ran when I was old enough to read, but the boy's name was "Toby", and Dad carried that nickname among his cronies for the rest of his life.

I have no recollection of those Wapella years, as I was only three and a half when Dad rented a farm of 240 acres on Maple Avenue to which we moved in March 1919. This farm was four and a half miles northeast of Wapella, and it was to be my home until 1932, my sophomore year in high school.

Of my first year on the farm I have memory of only two events. The first was when I was just past four and acquired my first dog "Herbert". I guess the dog acquired me, as it came to the farm uninvited and though my parents tried to discourage its staying, I insisted it was mine. That first year Dad had a hired man named Herbert, and he and I got along real well. When someone asked me the name of my dog, I immediately christened it "Herbert". Again I met discouragement from my family, but I stubbornly stuck to that name. Neither Herbert lasted too long. The hired man didn't care to labor much and only lasted one season, and Herbert the dog disappeared two months after presenting me with eight fine mongrel pups. My favorite pup, a brown male, with the reasonable name of "Brownie" somehow stayed behind when the rest "ran away". Brownie was my companion all through my school days on Maple Avenue.

Stories For My Grandchildren

The second memorable event was when I found bees could sting but didn't bother certain people – namely myself. My McCannon grandparents lived just a half mile west of us, and my mother took me with her one afternoon to visit them. Now their place was interesting. Farms in those days were rather small – usually 160 acres – but pretty well self sufficient. My grandparents had cattle, horses, mules and pigs. They also had turkeys, geese and chickens – the large Cochins and Plymouth Rocks. They had an orchard with apples, cherries, peaches and plums. They also had grape arbors, a large garden and a string of bee hives among the grapes.

This was a great place for a four year old to explore and have fun, until my mother heard a loud wail and rushed out to find me among the grape arbors with a swarm of angry bees bussing around me. Strangely none of those bees stung me, but when I sat down on a box to rest from my labors, I didn't notice that a bee already on the box was claiming residency. It stung! I yelled! That was the only sting I got, even though I had been poking a long slender stick through the holes in the hives and had a whole colony of very upset honeybees in a bit of frenzy around me.

After I had been enticed away from the lethal area and my one sting somewhat eased, my mother asked me what in the world I had been doing.

My reply was, "I was chasing the flies out of Grandma's chicken coops!"

I have to gloss over some of those early years on Maple Avenue because while my memory I could claim as impeccable, (elephants could take my correspondence course on total recall) either nothing remarkable happened or registered until I was well into Mooreville

Early Years

Grade School. I do remember I wasn't at all sure I wanted to go to school. Things were just fine on the farm.

Kelly Bishop came by one day in the spring to say that since we were to start school in the fall, the teacher had invited all prospective first graders to visit school the next day. I didn't go! My other sister and brother were both still in grade school – and dearly loved it – I wasn't sure I cared to give it a try. Nobody dragged me kicking and screaming to school that fall so I know my mother must have conned me into making a trial run of a few days. One thing about being suspicious of anything new is that disappointments were rare. As usual, I found that school was "just fine".

Before getting into my grade school days, I will describe Maple Avenue as it was when I was a child – a year or two on either side of that decade called the "Roaring Twenties". The road bearing that name stretched for two miles east and west with cross roads at either end. At the west end lived the Hales, the Longbrakes, and the Wilsons with Mooreville School occupying one corner. Two miles east was the Heidelberg School. The road itself was graded with ditches on either side. The road had no concrete, macadam or gravel. It was the dark brown fertile prairie soil of the area, which could and did produce fabulous yields of corn and equally fabulous yields of dust in the hot dry summers and knee-deep black mud in the wet days of winter and spring.

Beyond and above the ditches were blue grass banks for some fifteen feet to the fences that were usually hedges of Osage Orange. Wild gooseberries, raspberries and blackberries were mingled in the hedges and there were a few patches of wild strawberries or dewberries present. At regular intervals on the banks near the hedges were the ancient soft maple trees that gave their name to the road. These trees lined both sides of the road and except for providing a lofty abode for large flocks of crows and a few raccoons and squirrels, their main value was a certain pastoral beauty and areas of perpetual shade, as they nearly met to form a canopy over the dusty road in summer. Ten Mile Creek wandered throughout permanent blue grass pasture, crossed the Avenue a half mile east and continued through Moberly's pasture, running all summer fed by a number of cool springs.

Because hard surfaced roads were unknown in these rural areas, and no one had considered peeling back the rich topsoil to mine the deep gravel deposits, transport and travel through much of the winter and early spring months were restricted to horsepower or foot travel.

About every half mile, on either side of the road were the farm homes with barns, granaries, corn cribs, poultry houses and various other buildings. Every home had a garden, most had orchards and all had yards and plenty of shade trees.

There wasn't a modern house on the Avenue. Electricity wouldn't arrive on the Avenue for another fifteen years; there was no central heating, indoor running water or other amenities that we now take for granted. The large old iron cook stove in the kitchen burning cobs, wood and sometimes coal not only cooked the food but kept the kitchen warm in winter and sometimes unbearably hot in summer. It also was the only source of hot water. Sometimes in the hottest weather a kerosene oil burner was used, but it had to be located on the back porch as its smelly fumes were as disagreeable as hot iron cook stoves.

Early Years

A wood or coal burning stove in the living room kept that room passably comfortable on bitter evenings. Most bedrooms were unheated so heaps of blankets and comforters were essential. Fires went out at night so it was my job to bring in kindling, dry cobs and coal before dark so that the stoves could be fired early in the morning without having to gather the materials in the bitter mornings.

That was our routine, but not every home was the same. My cousin Roy told about going home with his buddies the Kinders after a basketball game when the temperature was near zero. He said the fires had long gone out, and there was no sign of fuel around. Harry, the old man, removed his good clothes and put on a pair of wool trousers, sweat shirt and wool sox. Roy said that was encouraging so he stayed bundled up until Harry could go out, bring in fuel and heat up things a bit. After Harry pulled on another sweater and a stocking cap, he proceeded to jump into bed and pull up the covers.

Before leaving the subject of Maple Avenue, I will mention what happened to it. The road is still there, and it still has the same name. Very little else remains that one could recognize as the environment of my childhood. On the last day or two of December 1924 and going into January 1925, we experienced the "Great Ice Storm". On that December at twilight, a light drizzly rain was falling. As the evening came on, temperatures dropped to below freezing, and the rain continued. Ice began to build up on fences, trees and structures.

The light rain continued all night and the weight of the ice increased. Fences sagged and broke. Shrubbery was flattened, and during the night there were loud reports as huge branches of the maple trees broke, and even some of the great maples split down the trunk under the crush of the ice. The next morning the clouds and rain had left and a bright eastern sun sparkled off a crystalline world that was for a few hours a diamond fairyland. One couldn't even ride a horse down Maple Avenue that day because of the tangle of trees covering the road. The ice and branches continued to fall during the day as the sun warmed the ice.

The next day it was safe to go out with axes and crosscut saws to clear the road. We had a model T Ford, and by jacking up the left rear wheel and attaching a belt and pulley to power a buzz saw, we piled up enough firewood to last us until the tornado of 1927. That cold winter morning presented us with a few hours of unforgettable crystal beauty but the havoc of stark splintered maples remained for years.

In April of 1927 while I was at Mooreville School, the tornado struck. We had windows on the north side but only a few high up to the south; so, our only warning was a darkening of the sky and a roar like a freight train. The teacher started to light kerosene lamps then thought better of it when tree limbs started sailing by the north windows. We saw the roof of Longbrake's barn sail off and their windmill topple over. Rain poured down in torrents, but in a few minutes it was all over, and we all went outside. Actually we were only at the edge of the storm. The center was a half mile east — just about where our home was. Every building at our place was flattened except our house.

Moberly's house across the road was moved off the foundation so they moved in with us for a few days while their house was repaired. No one on the Avenue was killed or even injured. We had a team of horses in our

Early Years

flattened barn, and near evening we found they were still alive. A hole was chopped through the roof, and with neighbors helping, a cross-cut saw was used to cut the fourteen inch beam holding them flat to the floor. We eventually led old Maude and Rex out through the hole in the roof. They were stiff and sore for weeks but recovered in time for the spring planting.

Again, firewood was all that was salvaged from the maples that survived the ice storm of two years earlier. Now the trees are all gone. The hedges have been pulled, fences moved out close to the ditches. The school house still stands but untenanted. The road has been blacktopped and Ten Mile Creek has been tiled out of existence. The bluegrass pastures have been plowed.

The names remain as do the nostalgic memories of those who lived there — particularly those whose "Long Long Thoughts" of youth coincide with that decade on the Avenue.

Mooreville

Several years ago when I was in active veterinary practice, a man and his wife brought a dog in for me to treat. The dog had a dermatitis and as I explained the possible cause and treatment, the wife rather questioned my suggested cause, whereupon the husband who hadn't said much up to that time said, "Now Honey, don't question the doctor. He's a graduate of the best school in the country."

At that I looked closely at the husband. I had not seen the dog before, had not yet asked their name and, so far as I knew, I had never seen either of them before. However, the reference to my school—Kansas State University—caused me to beam and say, "Don't tell me that you are a Kansas State grad too?"

"Naw, I mean you went to school at Mooreville," he answered.

Thirty five years earlier I had indeed carved my initials on various wooden structures at the one-room country school called Mooreville, and fully appreciated this astute scholarly institution of learning; but I was somewhat surprised to become reacquainted to another who shared this nostalgic memory. I stared at the gentleman for a while, then inquired, "Did you from time to time, when you were a short chubby fourth grader, display your talent for doing the Irish jig at school programs?"

He modestly admitted to this indignity. "Then," I said. "You have to be Wilson Green."

Now it isn't unusual to recognize someone you hadn't seen for that many years, except that I only went to school with this chap for about two years, and he was several years younger than I. I hadn't seen him since he was ten. However, the one-room rural school was unique. It was like part of the family. Everyone knew all about everyone else. Half of the youngsters were relatives or friends with whom you grew up, and the rest were few, and you knew them.

The fabled Little Red School house of the America of yesterday is looked back on as a nostalgic moment to a rural necessity of its day: A monument, however, to be eliminated as soon as progress would allow.

Yes, the one-room country grade school served its time on the prairies of Illinois in the nineteenth and into the first half of the Twentieth Century- where the snows piled deep in December, and the fertile loam soil made the roads a bottomless swamp with frequent thawing, or with the heavy rains of spring. Then, someone invented gravel roads! The country school, like the old spinning wheel and other useful memorabilia of their day fulfilled its purpose, then passed on to oblivion. We call it progress—and it is that—when we lay aside rude instruments— symbols of drudgery and hours of toil, for an easier, quicker, and more productive replacement.

There is, however, an ironic circle to most of this evolution of progress. When the farmer who had to cradle his wheat obtained his first McCormick Reaper, his scythe and cradle stayed where they fell, to moulder in a junk pile, or hung among the rafters in a little used shed. When the housewife no longer had to spin her own wool, the old spinning wheel was pushed back into the attic and forgotten. The same fate came to the ox-yoke when horse drawn steel gang plows came to turn the rough prairie sod; and in turn the single trees, the neck yoke, and other relics of the draft horse age were abandoned when the first tractors replaced the work horse. The users of these rude tools usually had no fond memories of such objects. They were the symbols of toil to be tossed aside with grim relief and forgotten—at least until the twilight of their lives, when the memory of their toil faded and was replaced by the nostalgia of their happy and robust youth.

A generation or two later all is changed. The grandchildren discover the obsolete cast off victims of progress—and find that they have resurrected art! The old cream cans, the butter churn, the hand-turned separator, the copper-bottomed boilers, the spinning wheels, the ox-yoke, and single trees are displayed as decorator items in rooms where they would never have been found in their day of usefulness.

However, it really isn't my intention to discuss the merits of old flatirons, copper boilers, or butter churns - either as useful tools, art objects, or as nostalgic memorabilia. The little old one room country school is my subject. Its day has passed. Most have burned, or have been torn down. Some have been made into residences. I am sure that if those that still stand were of considerable less bulk, they would have long ago found their way into someone's living room as a conversation piece.

Mooreville

No one would claim the little red schoolhouse as an art object. In fact here in central Illinois they weren't even red. Most were painted white. Rarely one was red, and a few weren't even painted. As a useful tool of its day, it served its purpose, however, and its contribution to the rural sociology of the Midwest can only be conjectured. It might be argued that the educational opportunities of rural America helped prevent a rural peasant class. There may be those who would say that because we had an independent and classless society, we had the schools. However, cause or effect as they may be—the rural one-room schools made their contribution.

But again, this is not intended as a philosophical treatise of country schools. This is about just one of them—Mooreville. I wouldn't consider myself an expert on them as a class, but Mooreville—yes! I spent nine happy years within those hallowed walls of learning and thereby qualify! Wait! Don't say it. I am well aware that there were only eight grades—but you see there was a little misunderstanding about fifth grade arithmetic—and our teacher Mrs. Armstrong, invited the entire class to repeat the fifth, to attempt absorption of academic trivia in 1926 that eluded us in 1925.

No stigma remained for anyone repeating a class. It was a common occurrence, and there were those who used up ten or even twelve years to negotiate the shoals of the eight grades in a country school. No one repeated merely one subject—he repeated the whole grade even though his weakness was in only one field. Seldom also were just one or two pupils held back. It was unthinkable to split up a class into two sections. The teacher was the entire work force for all eight grades, so her effectiveness dependent on her ingenuity of combining classes and keeping her talents from being spread too thin. In most years she taught only about five grades. First, second, and usually third were kept in order, but thereafter - especially if there were one or two in the grade—they bounced around a bit. A bright third grader might skip fourth, and join in with the fifth, or a less accomplished one might be held back to mingle in with the onrushing second graders.

Our class was large—seven in all, five boys and two girls. We weren't all the same age. We caught up with Mousie and Chink in second grade and were in turn overtaken by Willie in the fourth. All seven fell back then in the fifth. Come to think of it, Mousie should be the one describing Mooreville. He had the longest exposure. We lost him in the county examinations at the end of the seventh grade. He had two more years of residency after the rest of us left for high school.

You see, the culmination of these country school days came in May after the seventh and eight grades. The teacher paraded her students to the County Seat, where a series of tests prepared by the County Superintendent of Schools was administered to all rural students. We had to get passing grades in arithmetic, geography, English, U.S. and Illinois histories, and civics. The teacher ordinarily did not have both the seventh and eighth in the same year, so the last month of school were nervous days of constant review for that class she was trying to push upward.

Actually, most of the class, while deploring the constant review, was not nervous. We looked forward to a day in town, gorging ourselves on hot dogs and chocolate sodas, even with the less pleasant task of solving the questions on the exams. It was the teacher

Mooreville

who was nervous. Her own ranking depended to some degree on how well her class did; but mainly I am sure that no matter how delightful she found the wide-eyed innocents when they first came under her wing, after eight or ten years, the furrowed brow became unwrinkled, and audible sighs of relief were profuse when news came that this boy or that class negotiated the tests and would pass on to more advanced schooling.

Well, here I have gotten myself graduated and haven't really described what it was like in the one room country school. Nor have I described the lessons of life learned there. My life at Mooreville coincided with that decade of the "Roaring Twenties". We detected no roars along the pastoral setting of Maple Avenue and were perhaps a bit startled to learn at a later time of that sobriquet for those delightful school days.

Mooreville was so named—as such schools frequently were—for a certain Mr. Moore who donated about three acres of land for the purpose of a school. Moore was a business associated of David Davis, the Supreme Court Justice of Lincoln fame, and they later owned the farm together. Eventually, Judge Davis acquired the farm, but Moore's name stayed with the school.

The school rested at a crossroads on the west end of a shady country road called Maple Avenue. Two miles east, the Heidelberg School marked the east end of Maple Avenue. In between, the avenue was a dusty road in summer and a muddy road in winter when it wasn't frozen. On either side of the road beyond the ditches were wide grassy banks with ancient maple trees marching in ordered fashion, whose towering tops cast a perpetual shade over the road in summer. Beyond the line of trees, hedges of Osage orange fenced the orchards and pastures of the farm families.

The school districts were small in those days—rarely reaching for more than a mile in any direction from the school. This was because the kids all walked to school—even the first graders, who might have to trudge a mile and a half or more in bitter weather, if they lived at the more distant corners of the district. This was the day of the small farm, tilled by horses, so there were usually fifteen to eighteen families within the district. The farmers were young, usually rented the land, and larger families were the rule. Because of this we usually had from twenty to twenty-five pupils. Today this is all changed. The farm houses and farm families have disappeared. The farms have become consolidated like the school districts, and there are probably only two or three children of grade school age in this district where once there were twenty five.

Now after achieving the age of six, I was a bit put out to find that I was expected to go to school. Now I had nothing against school, but it was an unknown quantity and things were just fine with me in my world on the farm. I'm not sure just how my parents convinced me to give it a try, but rather grudgingly and suspicious, I went and found that school was just fine too. I knew my alphabet and numbers when I arrived there, but phonetics revealed words, and words opened up reading, and with reading all of education unfolded.

I believe it was the social structure of the one room school that made it both unique and of value. When there are children ranging from six to sixteen years in the same room with one mentor, not only teaching skills are necessary, but a proper and workable discipline is

Mooreville

imperative or chaos results. The school is rather like an extension of the family unit, or a bridge between the family and more specialized education. Every element that makes for a good family relationship existed in the school: discipline, cooperation, competition, assistance, and respect. The great weakness of the school was that so much depended upon the teacher, just as with the family so much depends upon the family head. We had excellent teachers at Mooreville.

The Bullies of the Seventh Grade

Now children are animals—just like the domestic or wild animals around us—and a definite pecking order is soon established in school, just as is established in the poultry flock, a wolf pack, or the cattle herd. The older, the stronger, or the smarter soon become dominate. This domination is somewhat modified if the weaker has an older and stronger brother or sister to protect him; and of course, there is always the teacher for arbitration. However, the teacher is usually there only as the ultimate arbitrator, and school kids soon discover it best to find and accept the social strata without recourse to teachers or parents. In the lower grades there were no visible efforts at dominating others but as the students moved up in grade or size, the gradual awareness of power inevitably crept in.

The boys rather fancied themselves as bullies, and the girls discovered the joy of plaguing the boys. I believe it was in fifth grade that three of the girls succeeded in exasperating Mousie, Kelly, and myself to the extent we resorted to doing battle with clods and rock-throwing. They, of course retreated squealing to the girls' outdoor privy. The battle continued, though of course, the area near the out-house was strictly out-of-bounds for boys. We soon found we were more

The Bullies of the Seventh Grade

strategically situated when I climbed a nearby tree and heaved debris over the board wall, being supplied by Mousie and Kelly from below. This proved to be our undoing as it allowed June—the swiftest—to escape and race to the school house to blow the whistle on us to Mrs. Armstrong.

We quickly retreated to the boys' side of the school ground and started playing ball, but Mrs. Armstrong soon had us inside and armed with a maple switch, she proceeded to give us a whipping. Mousie was first, Kelly's turn was next, and midway on my turn the switch broke. I think she was relieved to think the job was finished, and then went on to lecture us about how such misbehavior would bring continued pain to sensitive areas. Of course stubborn me had to put in, "Aw that didn't hurt!"

Up to that point, I think she was more amused than angry, but in a huff she quickly left the room in a very determined way. Kelly then blurted out very disgustedly, "Why'ja hafta say that for? We're really gonna get it now."

She returned shortly with a stouter cudgel and repeated the whole process. Mousie, Kelly, then me. That's real democracy; I lip off, so Mousie and Kelly get whipped too. This time she didn't inquire as to whether we felt it or not.

I always got a lot of pleasure out of that experience—at least after I found she didn't tell my parents. How could anyone go through country grade school without at least one spanking? Here I got two, both in the same day! And they really didn't hurt much!

The great day arrived in the fall of 1928. The "Tough Guys" were in the seventh grade. Hunger Karr and Buck Reynolds had graduated. We became the top dogs. Mousie, Kelly, Willie, Chink, and I assumed our rightful inheritance. The girls didn't count. We played endless baseball, basketball, shinny, and other roughhouse sports at recess and noon. We ate our noon lunch high up in the old box elder tree and kept the girls and smaller children on their half of the school grounds with their "hide-and-seek", "dare base", and "blackman" games. Only the oncoming boys of the fifth grade who accepted our rules joined us.

All this was fine, except that winter inevitably came on, and the cold and wet grounds chased us indoors. Now Mooreville was a relatively new and roomy school and had a full basement, although very low basement ceiling. We with clear reason expected to move our ball games down there. Mrs. Armstrong, however, with all the unreasonable stubbornness of one who didn't particularly care for physical education, ruled that since we governed the south half of the playground, we would have to be satisfied with the south half of the basement. The rest was reserved for child games, and a "play" store with bottles, cans, and other kid toys. It invariably happened that our errant basketball escaped and crashed into the "store" side. With the cry of "Mrs. Armstrong!", we always had to clean up the damage, and then had to spend the balance of the noon hour or recess in our seats upstairs.

This rank injustice provided us with many happy hours of plotting revenge. We were kept from forgetting those indignities by having our faults pointed out to us quite frequently. I recall the day I was sent to the basement during school to stoke the coal furnace. Now we wouldn't for a moment admit that this chore was

The Bullies of the Seventh Grade

anything but an imposition, but it was a fine way to waste a little time. You could usually use up about fifteen minutes, but you had to be alert to get ready to dash up the steps when you heard the teacher's footsteps approaching the basement door. On this occasion she must have had a long recitation, because I had time to heat the poker red hot and burn my initials in the ceiling beam. Now this wasn't very smart. I should have imprinted "JUNE". At any rate I never again was allowed to stoke the furnace.

Now the teachers of these country schools had an inexhaustible source of slave labor at their disposal. It was willing labor to clean the blackboards, dust the erasers, even sweep until you arrived in the upper grades. Then you had outgrown such things. It was especially irking to the seventh grade boys to have to clean up the basement on a particular Friday afternoon. It happened that we had been banned from the basement for a whole week because of some trivial mishap, and it was the fragile "store" area we had to put in order.

The reason for the cleaning was to get the school in shape for a district girls' meeting. The girls had a program of singing and elocution prepared for the mothers of the district on that Friday after school let out. Under the watchful eye of Mrs. Armstrong, we had to box up and store all the cans, bottles, glassware, and knickknacks, then sweep and scrub the basement we were banned from. Kelly, always the thoughtful type, got most of the bottles in one big box, and positioned it on the highest shelf adjacent to the basement window. We were told very gleefully by the girls that we could not hang around the school. We had to go home immediately. Now we wouldn't have stayed around anyway, but when we found we were ordered home, we decided to come back. We were great plotters.

Now Chink lived just across the road from the school, and he was always in trouble at home because June was his sister and usually pointed out his actions in school at the supper table. He declined to join us on this particular evening. Willie and Mousie started down the road north past the Longbrake farm. Kelly and I started east up Maple Avenue. Sure enough the teacher had two girls stationed outside to see if we actually left. Kelly and I went until we were hidden from sight by the hedge and alders, then we dropped down and crept back like Indians stalking a frontier stockade. We crouched and waited.

When Willie and Mousie went out of sight behind the Longbrake buildings, the girls decided all was well and disappeared indoors. Kelly and I darted back across the road to the shelter of the school building to wait for the others. I kept watching the north road but they did not return. Unbeknownst to us they decided they would be seen from the north windows, so had hiked clear around the Longbrake farm to come upon the school from the blind west side.

In the meantime Kelly had scouted around and came back with two good sticks. With one we managed to poke open the basement window and prop it open through the outside grill. The other reached the box very nicely. I was still urging Kelly to wait a little longer for Mousie and Willie, when we could hear June begin her song. Kelly decided this was the time, and the box toppled and hit the concrete floor with a splintering crash of broken bottles and clattering cans. The high note being attempted on "The Little Grey Home in the West" came

The Bullies of the Seventh Grade

to an abrupt halt, but not the two boys streaking toward Maple Avenue.

I dived into a shallow ditch and flattened out, and Kelly had just straightened up behind a rather small tree like a barn rat in a room full of weasels when Mrs. Armstrong came tearing through the door and dashed toward the rear of the school. She arrived at the back of the school just as Mousie and Willie unsuspectingly climbed over the back fence after a weary half mile hike.

When we next saw her, she had Mousie by an ear and Willie by the collar as she marched them indoors. Willie looked longingly in our direction, but manfully refrained from saying, "Hi Boys!" Kelly and I churned up Maple Avenue, eager to get at our evening chores.

Well, Willie and Mousie had to do another clean-up job.

I truly dreaded going back to school on Monday. To my great amazement school proceeded as usual. Mrs. Armstrong didn't even look at me suspiciously. The Code of Mooreville remained unsullied...

Skunk Hunting

Wild animals of the small variety were invariably present along Maple Avenue in the 1920's when I was a kid, but they were never so numerous as to be a nuisance. Wild rabbit, squirrel, raccoon, possum, fox and quail were familiar sights, but there was an ecological balance. When they were plentiful, some were hunted for food, and some hunted or trapped for their fur.

Skunk was a different situation. That animal is a member of the weasel family and dearly loves eggs and chickens. They had dens all over and under barns and if they could den up under a chicken house, they had it made. The skunk didn't run very fast – and he really didn't need to because that odiferous animal could fire a jet stream of musk with deadly accuracy into the eyes of any person or animal that was foolish enough to get within twenty feet of him. This musk was acid to cause a burning sensation and temporary blindness. It took a pretty dumb kid to let that happen, but if any dog or boy got close enough to catch any of that spray it stayed on for weeks, and in the case of clothes, they were frequently burned because they smelled of skunk. Because of this it was almost always open season on

Skunk Hunting

skunk but they held their own and were always numerous.

The fur of the skunk was used, but it was not very valuable. One mink was worth a dozen skunks so trappers didn't go much for skunk. One exception was Mulligan Karr, and he trapped everything. Many a day he came to school smelling of skunk – having tended his trap line before school. The teacher invariably sent him home, and it took a real odor for that to happen. That might have been part of the reason he ran the line because he didn't care much for school, but he sure missed plenty of school for that reason. We can't blame skunk for the fact that Mulligan never made it to the eighth grade, but it sure provided a few holidays for him.

However, the episode I had with the skunk happened in the summer time. I must have been in about the fifth or sixth grade and well acquainted with our common animals. On this particular warm sunny day, Billy Moberly, two years younger than I and my Hale cousins were with me in our gooseberry patch, trying to make ourselves sick eating green gooseberries. Wilma Hale, the youngest was closest to the road and screamed out, "There goes a snake!" Of course Billy and I, intrepid hunters as we were, grabbed clubs and assured the girls and smaller kids to stand back that we would handle this situation. We got through the hedge fence, but to our surprise we found not a snake but a skunk trotting down a rut in the middle of the Avenue.

Of course Billy and I attacked using what ammunition we had at hand – mostly sticks and clods of hard dirt but stayed clear out of range of the ammunition the skunk had. Billy was beyond the ditch on one side and I was on the other side and we sometimes scored but clods of dirt don't do much damage. This running battle continued for a long time, and we finally found we had chased the skunk all the way to the dooryard of the Longbrakes – across from Mooreville School. Here ammunition was more plentiful, and I found a brick that I heaved at and hit the skunk. As he doubled up, his scent glands were directed away from me and toward the Longbrake house so I dashed in and finished him off with a club and streaked off to safety.

I didn't get a drop of scent on me, but that dying skunk sprayed the Longbrake house from one end to the other. I knew the smell would linger for weeks so Billy and I decided we'd better get out of there. Unfortunately, Mrs. Longbrake came running out of the house before we could disappear, yelling, "What in the world is going on!"

I said, "Mrs. Longbrake, Billy and I saw this skunk and we thought it was trying to get your chickens so we killed it."

She said, "You mean you kids killed the skunk? You brave boys."

Well, we left for home right then. We didn't explain then or anytime afterward that we had chased that skunk for a half mile before getting it on the Longbrake doorstep.

The Rinkydinks

Kids were never bored on Maple Avenue in the 1920's. Nobody went to their parents complaining of having nothing to do. Far from it! If they did, there would have been a host of activities to engage in – rake the yard, clean out the hen house, hoe the garden, get fuel stacked up and on and on. Yes, every youngster had certain chores or duties from an early age, with increasing responsibilities and work as he grew older. Yet, I could not name one child within five miles of us who was overworked, mistreated or was an object of pity because of severe parents.

There were actually boys of near my age who looked forward to doing farm work – though I would hasten to add that I wasn't necessarily one of them. Most of these chaps weren't too keen on milking cows, cleaning out barns but looked forward to field work and other grown-up duties. I must have been just out of third or fourth grade on an early spring morning when my mother awoke me to say that Dad was going to let me drive a team on a roller than morning. She added, "Now wouldn't you like to do that?"

The roller or packer was the simplest of the horse-drawn machinery, with a single two horse team – usually the gentlest or oldest. It was a corrugated round iron

The Rinkydinks

gadget to break up clods and pack the plowed fields for planting or water conservation. Most kids got their first field experience on this implement, although milking cows, getting hay down from the haymow and feeding all the livestock began at an earlier time.

At any rate I do distinctly remember my mother waking me to ask if I wanted to run the roller. I also remember my reply, "No thanks. I'll just roll over in bed!"

I remember I was allowed to sleep on, but I also remember that by midmorning I was driving old Prince and Barney to the roller. I can't say that I got any great kick out of farm work, but since I was suspiciously pessimistic about the pleasures expected, I was never too disappointed and able to accept and endure it with equanimity.

Actually I started out to talk about the lack of boredom on the farm in my childhood. We, of course, had neither television nor radio though by the time I could read, we did have books. We did have space, the out-of-doors, and buildings where imagination could allow for amusement. I fought innumerable wars behind the farm buildings with the old useless pump engine for my artillery. After my grandfather took me to my first Tom Mix movie, I was a cowboy for years. And we did have companions – boys of my own age or a few years older and younger.

These were not daily companions- not even visitors of every other day. Billy Moberly lived across the road and we would play maybe once or rarely twice a week. Kelly was a half mile away and Chink and Willie were closer. My cousin Roy and Mousie lived two miles away. There were a few others at times but visiting was for summer months. During the school year recess and noon hour sufficed and anyways chores and homework took up most of the rest of the time.

Visiting and playing together was infrequent enough and companions so few that such occasions were completely enjoyed and there was no reason for disagreements. From the early days of games like Hide and Seek, barn climbing through the years when we were all cowboys (except a few of the younger ones who had to be outlaws or Indians), we gradually worked up to sports – of which baseball held pre-eminence.

While there maybe is some debate as to what the national sport of the United States is at the present time, there was no question during the decade of the 1920's. Baseball was THE sport. Every town, every village, every school played baseball. The rural area two miles north of Maple Avenue was called Irish Row and was inhabited by the Ryans, the Toohills, the Flaretys, the Carritys, the Burns, the O'Briens, the McGraths, the Learys. They had a good semi-pro team with a game every Sunday against some of the best town teams for thirty or forty miles around. I might add that the Irish Row Shamrocks were usually the victors. I went to many of these games and by the time I was in fourth grade, I realized that being a cowboy was a mistake and that being a professional baseball player was the only real profession. We played a lot of ball in school; and during the summer months whenever we could get time off from farm work, we tried to get enough boys together to work up some kind of game.

Now it happened that there was a comic strip in the daily paper under the name of Winnie Winkle; in fact, a version ran until recent years. However, in those days

The Rinkydinks

the strip was mostly about Winnie's brother Perry and his gang who played a lot of baseball and called themselves the Rinkydinks.

Perry, of course was the leader, and he had Spike as his main cohort with Shorty, a chubby catcher and Chink, a tall skinny first baseman. My cousin Roy, who was two years older than me, and who being the eldest, originated most of our ideas and escapades, decided we too would have a baseball team calling it the Maple Avenue Rinkydinks.

Quite naturally, Roy was the pitcher and named himself Perry. I was called Spike and being the second most skillful, I could pick any position except pitcher. "Shorty" Mousie and "Chink" Longbrake acquired permanent nicknames but Roy and I didn't keep ours. Roy laid the law down; we were all to acquire baseball suits and we had to have baseballs and some equipment. Of course when I brought the matter of uniforms up in my home, it was soon vetoed as my parents, having gotten me a glove for Christmas, made it clear that was the limit.

As a matter of fact, Roy wasn't successful either. His mother agreed to cut up a white flannel dress, but she never quite got it sewn into anything that looked like a baseball uniform. Only Chink Longbrake was able to convince his parents that everybody was going to buy their kids a uniform. Chink was a tall boy but far from skillful. In fact he could be counted on to catch only about one throw out of four. We played him mostly at First Base because he looked like the Chink of the Rinkydinks- and after all, he was the only well-dressed player on the field.

Well, this franchise operated for over two years, and I am happy to report we were undefeated during the entire life of the team. We even played a few games the second and third year.

You see it was tough to get nine kids together to play ball when we were allowed only about a half day a week to do so. Oh, we practiced a lot. We had a diamond measured out in Moberly's pasture, in our front barn lot, at Mooreville School and at Roy's; and while we practiced every chance we got all summer, we seldom had more than seven or eight boys together. For more than a year we practiced and plotted. We worked on every play we saw at the Shamrock's games, and we boasted of how we were going to beat the Salt Creek Timber Wolves, the Wapella town team and all the surrounding districts.

The second summer was only about half over when Roy announced that we had a bonified game scheduled. He had convinced Archie Taylor and Vachel Best that we were a bum team, and we would come over to their home grounds to play them one Saturday. The great day came and we paraded over to Ned Best's pasture to play the Progress School Bearcats. They could get a team together by using some of our younger and less skillful performers. I think we tried to make it a little less one-sided, but the best we could do was to beat them about 45-0.

Roy didn't let them off the hook and got them into another game a few weeks later after getting a couple of better players for them. Another cousin of mine, Louie Rolofson, and Warren Stevens were certainly an improvement for them, but they were still no match for us so they disintegrated as a team. We were without competition.

The Rinkydinks

Roy always had the intention of winning so the next summer while the old Rinkydinks practiced, he was of high school age. When he got a game lined up with some older and more able players around Heyworth, we played them and beat them badly, but only he and I were of the old Rinkydinks. Mousie, Chink, Shorty, Kelly, Willie, Bill weren't invited. Roy got the Greens, the Abels and the Kinders out of Wapella and even I was relegated to playing the outfield. I was the only one not in high school so there was no further mention of Rinkydinks.

My baseball years didn't end with the Rinkydinks. During my seventh and eighth grade at Mooreville, unencumbered by Cousin Roy and other older boys, I was top dog and pitcher and we played incessantly as the weather permitted.

When I entered high school at Wapella as a freshman in the fall of 1930, my parents would not let me come out for basketball because practice was held in the evening after supper; however, I was allowed to play baseball and played third base for Wapella High School. We had a good team because the Greens, the Kinders, the Abeles and Cousin Roy were upper classmen and skillful.

In 1932 during the spring of my sophomore year, my parents moved to a farm near Normal, Illinois and I transferred to Normal Community High – a school three or four times the size of Wapella. I played second base for NCHS that spring, but it was my last high school baseball since it was Depression time and baseball was taken out of the school as an economy move.

I claimed for years the only reason I didn't become a major league ball player was the fact that NCHS

Stories For My Grandchildren

couldn't afford to buy a few baseballs during my high school days.

The Horses on the Farm

As I have previously indicated, in my early years on the farm we were dependant on horses and not the horse power of the internal combustion engines. I was seven or eight years old when we owned our first automobile and that was a 1921 second hand Model T of rather questionable dependability. Even then there were several months of the year in which an auto was of little value. It was not until 1934 that we had our first tractor, although a few of our neighbors had Fordsons or Farmalls in the middle and late 1920's.

Rural America depended upon the horse for work, for travel, for communication and for pleasure from the time of opening new frontiers up through the early decades of the Twentieth Century. The dependence on the horse accounts for why we as omnivorous animals consume beef, pork, and mutton but not horse flesh. The last is just as tasty, as wholesome, and probably freer of disease and impurities, but one doesn't place on the table one's pets or family retainers. The need fulfilled by the horse also accounts for the many stories of loyalty and intelligence of man's "Noblest Friend" – most of which are largely exaggerated.

Our first horse with which I had an intimate acquaintance was old Prince. When we moved to the farm in 1919, I rode with my mother in a spring wagon behind Prince and Barney. Prince though not young was a pretty good horse and gentle, but Barney was an ugly jug-headed mongrel. Barney worked just well enough to miss being sold to the "Fox Farm" but only barely. Field work continued until 6 p.m. during the busy seasons, but Barney seemed to quit about 5 o'clock. When he decided it was quitting time, you couldn't move him unless he was headed toward the barn and the evening feeding.

Prince was a light "road horse". He could be ridden as a saddle horse, driven alone by my mother in a buggy or worked in the field on less than the heaviest work. I was probably seven or eight and Prince was probably past twenty when he became my main means of transportation. He was somewhat spavined, limped a lot, and used very little except by me. I could approach him in the pasture to pet him, feed him apples and hold on to his mane, but not if I had a bridle in my hand. If I needed his service, it was a game of wits. I had to approach him with a rope hidden in my overalls or appear to be after other animals and snare him by accident.

If he suspected I was trying for him, he would trot around the pasture like a race horse with his tail in the air. After forty-five minutes or more and I finally caught him, he wouldn't give me any trouble but would limp piteously all the way to the barn. We had great times trying to outfox each other. When I was too small to climb up on his back, he would stand quietly along side a fence or box then when I would start to climb up, he would absent-mindedly shift around just outside my range. I sometimes out smarted him. One trick I learned was when I managed to catch him in the pasture and get

The Horses on the Farm

a bridle on, I would lead him to some lush grass where I would pause. He would invariably lower his head to graze, and I would jump on his neck. His head would snap up and I would slide down to his back.

We had other better roadsters. Dean and Slocum were of racehorse breeding. They were good saddle horses and used to pull surreys or wagons and planted our corn. However, the best riding horses we had were Mary Legs and her off-spring. Dad bought her at an American Saddle Horse dispersal sale. He got her for very little money — thirty-five dollars I believe, because she was undersized. She was a delight to ride. I rode her daily to and from high school when I was a freshman. It was a four and a half mile trip each way. By that time she had produced the first of her four foals. Silver Legs was as great as her dam. She was half Arabian, fast and tireless but like a rocking chair to ride. By the time I was twelve, I broke and rode all of our horses whether they were for riding or not. Mary Legs produced three more colts for us. King and Queen were bays and good enough workers but poor saddle horses. Beauty, a brown mare, was like Mary Legs and Silver Legs. She was gentle and a comfort to ride. I rode her when she was less than two; and while she was spirited and likely would give a few playful pitches when you first got on her, you could nap under her and never get stepped on, kicked or bitten. She only embarrassed me once.

Some city cousins visited once from Chicago and while they were fascinated by all farm animals, they particularly wished to see someone ride a bucking bronco. Of course I let them know we had just such a wild bronco. I saddled Beauty and led her out. Of course none of them would get aboard so I told them to stand clear and watch me. I swung up into the saddle and since Beauty hadn't been ridden for several days and was full of beans she began her playful bucking. I couldn't quite locate the right stirrup and lost my balance so went over her head on about the second pitch. She never pitched me off before or since, but the indignity was that the saddle horn hooked my trousers and they ripped so that when I hit the ground, I was without any pants. Beauty stopped, put her nose down to me and looked soulfully as through to say, "Gee, I'm sorry. Did I get too rough?"

Beauty and Queen were the last horses my Dad had. They lived to reach the ripe old age of about thirty, with the last dozen years in retirement.

Of course we had many heavy draft horses used for heavy farm work. Old Deck, Bally, Rex and Bothwell were great pullers; and we had intermediate pullers – Maude, Nellie, Pet. Pet and Dan were part Clydesdale with white feathering on their legs. Both were foals from Nellie and both were high strung and would run away any chance they got. Dad had the first runaway with Pet and Rex when a train whistle startled them while he was pulling a load of corn near the elevator at Birkbeck. I had my first runaway when Pet was three and Dan was two. I was about twelve and was cultivating corn in the back forty. I had tied them to a hedge fence and left to walk about a hundred yards down the hedgerow to get a jacket I had left and did notice a "Dust Devil" in the field to the west. This whirlwind kicked up a spout of whirling dust and corn leaves and evidently hit the team. When I turned to come back, no horses were to be seen. I ran back and through a break in the hedge, I could see our barn and my brother untangling what was left of the cultivator.

The Horses on the Farm

I had another runaway with them a year later when I was heading to Wapella with a load of corn. Dad was with me as he was going to catch a train to Champaign to see a football game between Illinois and Army. As I went around a corner, a wheel dropped down where there was a washout and broke. The load of corn and Dad upset in the ditch and Pet and Dan tore down the road with what was left of the running gears. Nelson Thorpe caught them two miles down the road. We got Dad to the station on time, and it took my brother Dean and me quite a time to clean up the corn. Not too long afterward, I was again cultivating corn when a hamstring on Dan's collar broke, and they were again in full gallop. That time I kept my seat and managed to bring them under control, just plowing up about a hundred feet of green corn.

The team was finally broken up several years later when Lehman's Dairy saw Dad, and since they bought good horses for their dairy wagons, they made a good offer and Dad sold him for enough to buy a team. A few months later Dad was at a blacksmith shop and saw a Lehman wagon being repaired. Dad told the smithy he bet he could tell him what horse smashed the wagon. The smith verified that Dan was the horse and told Dad that he was glad he had sold Dan to Lehman's as he kept the smith busy on wagon repairs.

The last time I saw Old Dan was several months later, and he didn't look so spunky. He was plodding along the streets without a driver, stopping where he was supposed to and paying no attention to the city noises. He served Lehman's until the horse drawn milk wagons gave way to the motor delivery.

Stories For My Grandchildren

The Crime Wave on Maple Avenue

In the 1920's, farmers ordinarily worked in the fields from about 7 a.m. to 6 p.m., with an hour off at noon for feeding, watering and resting horses. This was with weather permitting during the busy months of plowing, planting, cultivating, hay making and harvest. Of course the family arose earlier – somewhere near 5 a.m. to finish the morning chores, have a large breakfast and harness up for the days work. Six p.m. was a fairly rigid quitting time, not necessarily just to permit the evening milking and other chores, but it was about the maximum to expect of the working horses. The less busy winter season, after the corn was picked, allowed a much shorter day.

This was the usual practice on Maple Avenue, except on the sixth day - Saturday, 4 p.m. was quitting time. Saturday night almost every family hurried through the chores to get to town. Town was Clinton, the county seat, about ten miles from Maple Avenue.

Here, on The Square, the Model T's were parked and neighbors who were perhaps only a half mile apart on The Avenue visited each other for the only time during the week. Groceries and other supplies for the upcoming week were purchased, and people strolled The Square to see who was in town and who wasn't and why. Usually

The Crime Wave on Maple Avenue

the town band played on the courthouse lawn. Kids of my age usually got a quarter for the week's work and were able to take in a cowboy movie at the old "K" Theatre and enjoy a hamburger afterwards. A quarter went some distance in those days!

On more than one occasion, on these Saturday nights, I heard my Dad mention, "Well, there's no one home anywhere on Maple Avenue; some of these times someone is going to bring a couple of trucks in and clean out the whole Avenue."

They never did! There wasn't a house on the Avenue that could be locked when the residents were away- and few that could be locked from the inside when they were home. Of course barns and other buildings had no security at all. I rather looked forward to that event occurring that my Dad had forecast, though at a much later time, it did occur to me that there probably was nothing much worth stealing in any of the houses along Maple Avenue. Oh, there were pigs, cattle, horses, grain and poultry: but the only cattle rustlers or horse thieves that I experienced were in the movies or the Western pulp magazines.

Nevertheless we did have one period of anxious excitement during the winter of 1926- I believe it was. On that winter day, a Saturday, with the roads wet and impassable for autos, my Uncle Arch Hale hitched a horse to a buggy and started to Clinton with some eggs and two cans of cream to market. In the Prairie Center area, about halfway to town with Uncle Arch halfway dozing and Old Nellie plodding along, out from behind a tree, a rather large black man stepped and called out to Arch, "Say Bo, will you sell me a cup of milk?"

Stories For My Grandchildren

Now to say that Uncle Arch was timid would be to put it mildly. He was of slight build, lame from the time his horse, Dick, fell with him shattering his leg and reluctant to venture out after dark without company. In addition I am sure he never knew or ever conversed with anyone of another race. There were a couple of popular black families in Clinton, but I don't think there was ever a black person before seen in the rural areas near Maple Avenue. In any event Uncle Arch did not choose to chat with the gentleman or investigate his intentions. He did manage to blurt out, "I don't have any" as he brought the whip down on the startled Nellie and got her into a brisk trot down the muddy road. Neither did Uncle Arch return to explain that it was sour cream, not milk in the cans.

What Arch did do was to hurry through with his errands in Clinton and hurry back home to get old Nellie unhitched and stabled before dark. Back indoors, he proceeded to call most of his neighbors on the party phone to see if any had been through the Prairie Center area, had seen or had had any contact with the rather large black person.

Considerable interest and plenty of speculation was forthcoming along the Avenue, though Arch was the only one that had seen the man. Someone suggested that the person was obviously on the lam since he lurked behind hedges and was hungry. Someone else suggested he was spying out the land for some gang. By the time the theories were all voiced, it was well past dark. Arch had interrupted his phoning long enough to get a hammer and nail down all the windows on the ground floor, but there were very few after dark chores performed that night. Burl Hickman had only one cow to

The Crime Wave on Maple Avenue

milk and he wasn't going out to do that. Coveys said they had turned the calves in to do their milking. Burl said his calf was tied in another stall so it would have to go hungry and the cow unmilked that night. Doors that had never been locked were latched, and if they could not be locked - had chairs wedged under the knobs.

The next day, Sunday came and went without any reported violence and no known losses of livestock. Chores were all performed well before dark and at least with the Hales, all expeditions outside the house were family projects. Certain security improvements with hammer, nails and boards were also accomplished. But Sunday and Monday passed without further alarm. Monday evening at just about dark, Burl Hickman called neighbors to say that Roy Rolofson, my cousin, and Andy Wilson had just stopped in to tell him they had seen a rather large individual on foot cross Maple Avenue and disappear into a field leading to Nate Foley's barn. Tuesday, Andy reported following footprints from behind Heidelburg School westward till he lost them near Ten Mile Creek.

The situation was obviously becoming more sinister so the local law came in to play. The local law was in the form of Walter Bishop, Kelly's dad, who was the duly elected township constable of some four or five years. I think he received a yearly stipend of some eighty dollars, which was clear profit since he had never been called on except once to find the owner of a strange horse that had turned up.

At any rate, at noon on Wednesday, Walter came to our place wearing his badge of office, carrying a shotgun, a rifle and a pistol and asked Dad to go with him to explore Nate Foley's barn. The way Walter summed it up was "that fellow had been in the neighborhood for five days and was up to no good." He wasn't in any of the buildings near houses so the only shelter he could find was the Foley barn. It was away from all homesteads, and the one time he was seen he was going in that directions and tracks led that way.

Dad said, "Sure, I'll go with you, but I don't think we'll find him there."

I think Walter would have liked to have gotten up a full posse, but his neighbors indicated that this was what they had elected him for so Dad being an old crony was the only one to go with him. They were gone for a couple of hours, rather anxious hours for me; but they found no evidence that the barn had been occupied. At this time Dad suggested that they go up and talk to Monte. Now Monte was my Uncle Monte Rolofson, Cousin Roy's dad.

The furor of the black invasion on Maple Avenue subsided and faded away. Somewhere there was a large black gentleman who probably found his way back to his normal environment, blissfully unaware of the number of interrupted milkings and nailed window sashes he caused.

As for me, I was disappointed. I was disappointed that cousin Roy hadn't enlisted me in helping perpetuate the mystery of sightings, footprints and the mysterious stranger stalking the neighborhood.

The Haunted House

Down on Maple Avenue, when I was a kid, we didn't really believe in ghosts. That didn't mean older kids wouldn't try to scare the young kids by telling ghost stories or inventing lurid stories of haunted houses and wild adventures. None of us kids believed it, of course, but such make-believe made for adventure and imagination.

We had haunted houses because every house closed up where no one lived was considered to be haunted. Up by Heidelberg School there was such a house. We kids sneaked into it, always in daylight, but as the house fell into greater disrepair, we lost interest. How could you imagine ghosts when you could see the whole interior from the road?

However, my favorite haunted house was about three miles from home and only a short distance from the home of my cousin Roy. Roy was two years older than I and imbued with a lively imagination. On several occasions when I went to his house, we would sneak down to play near the haunted house. Sometimes we would imagine the house full of outlaws and we thought we could see loopholes in the walls and while I could never quite see it, Roy was sure he could see a rifle barrel from time to time. We fired countless cap pistols at the house and sneaked up and circled it, calling for the outlaws to surrender. They never did.

At other times we were after the spooks, particularly if it was near dusk. Roy must have had good eyesight because he constantly spotted ghosts. I had more trouble, but as it grew darker even I could see mysterious shadows in the outside cave or at the upstairs windows. We scouted and skirmished around on many occasions, but I don't think we ever had nerve enough to enter and explore the house.

Several years later, long after growing beyond my gun-fighting years, I chanced to be near this haunted house again. In fact I was a freshman in high school. Our freshman basketball team had traveled to DeWitt for a game one night, and it was very late when we started back home. It was a dark night, and as with boys of all ages, everyone was willing to adventure when the subject of haunted houses came up. Chink Longbrake was driving the Model T we were in; Kelly Bishop, Willie Wilson, Jimmy Abel and I were passengers. The questions of personal bravery arose, and Kelly was pleased to announce he would be glad to explore any haunted house at midnight though unfortunately there seemed to be a housing shortage of the ghoul infested type, right at the moment.

I'm not absolutely sure Kelly was pleased, but all the rest seemed happy, when I announced I had just the house in mind for those who enjoyed nothing better than a midnight ramble among the bats and spooks. That this house was ideal was self-evident because it was not too far away from where we were and there were no habitations nearer than a half mile of the house; that it

The Haunted House

was haunted I could attest to, having seen numerous ghosts there when I was a little kid.

We parked the Model T in front of the house and a certain hesitation resulted because a dark house on an isolated road at midnight was not exactly the kind of fun thing freshmen boys looked forward to. But courage won out, except Kelly insisted someone go with him to prove he explored the house. Willie was the smallest and didn't choose to go. Chink insisted he was driving and had to be ready in case flight was indicated. Jimmy Abel suddenly admitted to having a headache so I was elected to go with Kelly. After all, it was my house; I was supposed to know all about it.

Kelly and I crept like Sioux Indians up to the house, circled it and went over the creaking sagging back porch. Hopefully the door would be locked but it wasn't. Bravely we pushed the door open and found ourselves in the black kitchen. Kelly dug in his pocket and brought out a handful of kitchen matches we would need to find our way around.

Kelly scratched and lit the first match and we stood petrified! There on the kitchen table were the dirty dishes and leftovers from the evening meal. Somebody had moved in and was living in the house. Kelly snuffed out the match and whispered, "Let's get out of here!"

No grass grew under my feet as I tore out of there, but I have to admit Kelly was twenty feet ahead of me when I vaulted over the fence. Chink leaned out the door and exclaimed, "Boy, I wouldn't believe any spooks were there but the way Kelly's traveling, there must be several!"

High School Daze

In September 1930 I began not only a new decade but my high school days at Wapella. Unlike my grade school days, I looked forward to high school with confidence and pleasure. It being a small school, only from 75-90 students, I already knew the greater share of my classmates and those in the upper classes.

I wasn't acquainted with Geraldine Ross, the best student in school, and was rather surprised to learn she was my steady girl friend. This was a product of my cousin Twila Rolofson who was imbued with a lively imagination and an arranger much like my other cousin, Roy Rolofson. Geraldine was Twila's best friend, and she thought we were suited to each other so it was an accomplished fact. Though Geraldine was my "Steady" from that freshman year, I never actually had a date with her. I walked her home from school once or twice though not completely as her father Arby Ross discouraged boys hanging around; I left before reaching her home. I did ask her for a date along toward spring. I heard the rumor that Evan Frazer was getting interested in her so in study hall when Geraldine went to sharpen a pencil, I nerved myself to whisper to her, "Would you care to go to the "Ag" picnic with me?"

High School Daze

She whispered back, "I surely would". So I beat Evan out. I had no idea how I was going to transport her to Weldon Springs where the picnic was held each spring; but that problem was solved when the school cancelled the event.

Actually athletics held priority over high school romances; I was more interested in baseball and basketball, the only sports at Wapella. I didn't get to come out for the teams as I had to get home for evening chores. Basketball practice was after supper and since I rode Mary Legs to school, I couldn't get back for practice. I did play on the "Ag" team and when spring arrived, my Dad relented and I came out for baseball. I made the team as a third baseman, and we had a winning team with the Kinders, the Abels, the Greenes and of course my Cousin Roy.

When my sophomore year rolled around, I not only played baseball but was allowed to come out for basketball. Our reserve team was all sophomores: Jimmy Abel, Paul Ives, Static McCastle, Kelly Bishop and myself. We played the first game at night and dressed and substituted for the varsity since the varsity consisted of only five of the best of the upper classmen. Both teams won most of their games and when the County Tournament was held, both our Varsity and our "Second" team won the championships.

Right after the county tournament, we went to Weldon to play two games, and only had ten players. Spud Kinder, Guilty Duncan and Jim George were ineligible. Larry Wade, our coach was also principal so he waited until after the county tournament before he announced the first semester grades. I didn't get to play in the first game; I was the lone sub on the bench. Static,

Paul Ives and I played the varsity game. We won both games. The next game was at Argenta, a pretty good team, and we lost the varsity game. Spud, Guilty and Jim made up work by this time and regained their eligibility so we sophomores reverted back to the Reserves.

Now it is the year 1932 and we were in the Great Depression. Things were tough. Dad rented a larger farm, 370 acres at Normal, Illinois; so on March 3, I drove old Maude and Rex hitched to a wagon of corn (with my riding horses, Mary Legs and Silver Legs tied to the back) the thirty miles to the new home near Normal. The next day I presented myself at Normal Community High School to finish out my sophomore year. There was no problem except they didn't teach agriculture at NCHS so I finished up the semester in woodworking. I knew absolutely no one there; it was four times the size of Wapella High. The students were mostly "town kids"; very few were from "the farm".

A few weeks later the baseball season started and I came out. I made the team as a second baseman. I think it was because of my uniform. NCHS hadn't spent money on uniforms for thirty years. I had my own uniform from the sandlots of Chicago- courtesy of my Chicago relatives, complete with cap and blue and white sox. It was so old it still had a collar on the blouse, but I was the best dressed player on the team. We didn't have a great team, primarily because we lacked a catcher who could hold Shearer, our captain and pitcher. Anyway, here I was a few weeks away from the farm at Wapella and already a letterman for NCHS. A few years later when Shearer was the property of the Brooklyn Dodgers and Bill Conroy of Trinity High was catching for the Boston

High School Daze

Red Sox, I could boast, "Shearer, yes he was my baseball captain; and when Conroy pitched for Trinity, I drove in the first run against him and singled twice off him at Old Fans Field."

Well, with this auspicious start at NCHS, I could hardly wait for the fall football season to start. Now I had never seen a high school football game, but I weighed about 138 pounds and considered myself pretty tough. Besides, if I didn't come out for football, I would have to walk the two miles home after school and milk about six cows and do other sundry chores. Sure I'm going out for football.

Of course by this time I had quite a few pals in school. Al Bohrer, Cy Stephens and Red Hoffman were coming out for football for the first time. When they asked me what position I was trying out for I said, "Oh, any place will do. What positions are available?"

Al who knew a lot about the game said, "Well, with your size you should be a backfield man, but you're way too slow. You're too small for the line so maybe you should try out for end."

"Yep," sez I, "that's what I had in mind. I'm out for End."

It didn't really matter what I came out for as we first-time out scrubs didn't get a chance to try any position. We only had one coach, Bob Prince, and he coached all the sports. He didn't look beyond the first two teams. He had everyone run two laps around the field then he selected his proposed starters from about twelve lettermen and his reserve team were experienced players he recognized. They then scrimmaged until it was time to run another two laps and go in. Al, Cy, Red and I along with another half dozen scrubs lay around the sidelines until some of us sneaked in the orchard west of the field and brought back apples for the group. We had to be careful for if the Coach saw us, we would have to run some extra laps. This went on all week: run two laps, sneak some apples, run two laps and go in. I didn't learn any football, but I was sound on apples! It wasn't too glamorous, but I thought it maybe a little better than going home and milking all those cows.

The second week started on Monday with a cold constant drizzle, not heavy but lasting all day. The football players asked the coach if practice was cancelled. He roared back, "No! You all need work, and anyway you'll have to play sometime in the rain."

Well, some of the lettermen decided they weren't going out to mess around in the mud and cold rain, but most did show up. Why the simple-minded scrubs showed up when nobody would miss them, I don't know; but I had a problem. It was either a chilling rain or rest my head on the wet flank of a bunch of Jerseys. Loyalty to the noble game of football won out!

Well, the coach was in the worst of moods. The team was not at all enthusiastic and too many were missing. Finally after excusing two or three more players, he ran out of reserves so growled over our way, "Hey, I need a left end. Any of you scrubs an end?"

Cy and Red pushed me up, "Hey, Mac, here's your chance; he's calling for you."

The first week of football had taught me a few things. I was sound on apples! I could write a treatise on the delicate difference in taste between the Northern Winesap and the Red Delicious; but on football, I would have profited just as much had I been on a safari in the Congo. I didn't know the rules or the principles of the game; but I did observe that it seemed popular to attempt mayhem on the opposing team's ball carrier.

At that point that was all I knew about football. Now in addition, I was wet, cold and miserable and welcomed a bit of physical action; so when the Coach sent Jack Snoddy, our best ball carrier around my end, I nailed him for a loss. Play after play when Jack or Curley Stagner came off right tackle or right end, I mowed them down. In retrospect, I know the blocking was not only uninspired, it was downright shoddy, but after about a dozen plays with the varsity unable to make any ground at my end, the Coach knowing his varsity coaching couldn't be at fault, came to the conclusion that he had untapped talent he didn't know about. In fact he was heard to say, "Hey, this guy is an End. Where has he been?"

He didn't even remember I was his second baseman the previous spring.

Well, all my buddies among the scrubs assured me that I had it made, and I was not only on the squad but I would be doing lots of playing. Tuesday night was dry and I stayed out of the orchard and paced up and down trying to look tough and ready for action. It was all in vain! With everybody back, I didn't get in any scrimmage either with or against the varsity. Wednesday night the same. I tried to look ready and eager, but no scrimmage. I was completely disillusioned.

Thursday night we had no contact practice, just ran through signal drills, and the coach passed out the first team jerseys. The eleventh orange and black jersey went to McCannon – left end! Boy, I was floored.

The next night, Friday, I was even more floored when Coach Bob Prince announced the starting lineup. I was starting at left end! I had never been in on the Varsity's play in scrimmage, and except for that wet Monday, I had never been in a play against them.

I know I should have gone to the coach and said, "Gee, thanks Coach but I don't know anything about football. I've never even seen a game. How about later when I've learned something?"

Of course I said nothing. Who knows, maybe I'm better than even I think I am. So I think that I set some kind of record; I started the first high school football game I ever saw, without ever running a practice play with the team and knowing absolutely nothing about the game.

Even more remarkable, he left me in for three quarters of the game. I guess I stayed in the game because nobody on our team was doing very well. When we had the ball and a play was called, I would ask Earl Phillips the tackle next to me what I was supposed to do. His answer was usually, "Block that tackle."

After I was told who my opponent was I got by as we didn't have a very sophisticated offense. On defense, I was more confident. After all I had scrimmaged for some fifteen minutes against our varsity on a muddy rainy night. And I did make a few tackles; however, the other team started running their plays around our right side, and I would rush in only to find the action on the other side of the field, and I couldn't overtake them.

Well, once when they started left, I slid behind the line and tackled the ball carrier over around our right end position. That was a mistake! The opponent coach saw what happened, and that's when I learned about reverses! The next time I slid behind the line, the ball was handed off to a wingback and he reversed and came through my vacated left end spot for a big gain. What a dirty trick to play on a country boy in his first game!

At that point the third quarter ended and Dick King, a letterman, came in to replace McCannon. That was to be my last start of the season. I continued on the traveling team and learned a little bit of football. I only got into games late when they were lost or our players were too battered. Prince put me into the Morris game at guard when they were running over our middle. Phillips told me I was doing great. I never got my hands on the ball carrier as I was always at the bottom of the pile, but that provided an obstacle for the ball carrier. I also played the last quarter at End against LaSalle-Peru, probably the best team in the state, when our Ends left limping off the field. I didn't win a letter my junior year, but it was some recompense to have Earl Phillips pull me to my feet saying. "Great going Mac, nice tackle" after I had shaken the stars from my head after nailing the 180 pound speed merchant from Peru.

I came out for basketball when the football season was over. I didn't really cut it at NCHS. I started the reserve game against Bloomington and caught a vicious elbow in the nose. I bled like a stuck pig, and my nose pointed toward my right ear. The doctor got the bleeding stopped after appreciable time and got the nose pointing straight ahead again, but I just made the traveling squad with little playing time after that.

The worse time though came in the spring. As an economy move the school dropped baseball. I always claimed that was all that kept me out of the big leagues; the school couldn't afford to buy a dozen baseballs for the season.

Bob Prince was fired as coach that spring and Hap Arends came in to coach. I never blamed Prince for anything. He never degraded me, but he really didn't teach me much. I learned on my own. My senior year we lost all the big boys on our team. The Phillips boys, Bearden, Curley Stagner were all graduated, but we had Hap and he taught us football. We were small, not very talented, but we learned how to play the game and had a good season. I played left end most of the season but shifted to guard for the Pontiac game as our guard ranks thinned out and played the last game at right tackle.

I assisted Hap in basketball but didn't play. I coached his freshmen, refereed the reserve games, ran Hap's intramural program and scouted for him.

All in all, my senior year was successful and happy after my disappointments with my junior year. I didn't need or get much study hall time. Jack Stoltz, our principal, called me in to say he noticed I didn't need much study time and wondered if I wanted to spend that hour in his office to answer phone calls and other such sundry duties. I was flattered and didn't realize until much later that was Jack's way of getting my disruptive presence away from the study hall.

That job lasted until one day my buddy, Louie Poston, called to say, "Mac, this is Louie Poston's mother, and Louie isn't well and won't be in school today." I should have known better. Louie was a Victory Hall boy and didn't have a mother in town so I went back to study hall until they put me in as student librarian.

Jack Stoltz was a very fine principal and ran a "tight" school. There was no boisterous noise or running in the halls, and if someone banged a locker, Jack would stick his head out of his door and the pained look on his face froze everyone. I think he must have practiced that pained expression for hours before a mirror because he sure got a lot of mileage out of it.

The study hall on the third floor served as cafeteria for those of us who brought our own lunch. During the noon hour it came in for a little horseplay and some noise. Jack called me, Louie and Babe Griffin aside one day to tell us it appeared certain elements were causing a bit too much noise and disturbances; and he was thereby appointing us as monitors to insure that the proper level of decorum was maintained during the noon hour.

Of course we accepted the responsibility; we would enjoy enforcing anything. For days we kept on the lookout for anyone creating a disturbance so we could put it down. Nothing happened and the hall was serene. We finally looked at each other and arrived at the conclusion that Jack had conned us again. We were the ones he wanted us to regulate!

Well, high school was a great place and a great experience. Every day was a fun day, but that particular facet of my life was to end in June 1934. I was in the senior class play and in the National Honor Society besides my librarian and monitoring duties. I was the recipient of the Harold Osborne Trophy, awarded to the letter athlete with the highest scholastic standing.

College lay ahead of me; in fact two college graduations were to be my lot, but my days in Mooreville (the country grade school), Wapella High and Normal Community (even above the knowledge acquired) would impart an experience to be looked back on with nostalgic thankfulness.

The Great Depression

This is not intended as an economic treatise on The Great Depression of the 1930's. Economists and fiscal experts have written a great deal on it, and I most assuredly do not claim to be in the same class with them. I am merely recounting my experiences of that time since it covered my high school and first college years.

I could sum it up by saying that The Depression had no great effect on me and left no lasting scars on me or my family. In looking back after much time had elapsed, I could even say it was of considerable educational benefit and an experience that I am glad to have gone through. It was a normal life of the times and while there were certain privations, we hardly knew at the time that we were going through anything catastrophic. We were in the same boat as nearly everyone we knew. In rural Illinois we saw no anarchy, crime, hunger or suffering. We suffered no great financial setbacks since we had no wealth before, during or after The Depression years; we had adequate food, clothing, housing and no one to be envious of.

On the farm, The Depression began long before the Stock Market Crash in 1929. It began with the "Good Times": rising economy, inflation, higher prices and

The Great Depression

expanding industry and transportation after the First World War. Farmers who had made money and saved some capital went into debt buying land at inflated prices in the early 20's. They didn't pay much down and paid the interest and on the mortgage principal through the 1920's then found they still owed more for their land than what it would sell for. Some held on and eked through but many more went bankrupt.

My Dad never had enough capital to buy land and only borrowed to buy horses and equipment when he started farming. In the middle twenties, we were used to corn selling for a dollar a bushel, and a few years later after a good crop (possibly 1928) corn prices dropped drastically so Dad fixed up more crib space and held over his crop to the next year. Prices continued to drop and he finally had to sell for much less than he could have gotten a year earlier. But, he still had grain to sell and prices on many or most things were down also so while we had to do with less, we were not destitute.

Earlier in recounting my childhood, I mentioned my Grandfather McCannon's rented farm (just 160 acres) and how self sufficient it was. Our farming during my childhood and school days was nearly as self sufficient. We never had to buy milk, cottage cheese, cream or butter. We had poultry so we had fried chicken most Sundays all summer, roast chicken the rest of the year and never bought eggs. We had a lot of pork; when November came, farmers got together and had their hog butchering. We had our own bacon, ham, sausage and surplus of lard for cooking.

We had no electricity or gas so had no such utility bills. Our water was windmill or hand pumped. My mother's garden kept us in fresh vegetables all summer, and she canned green beans, peas, corn by the scores of jars and made apple butter, plum butter and grape juice. Several times I can recall her making her own soap. We ground our own horseradish and had turnips, parsnips and carrots as well as onions most of the year. We did have to buy salt, sugar, (we had no beehives) flour, spices, kerosene for our lamps and gasoline for our Model T (and later our other Fords) but that didn't take much if you stayed home.

I even recall Dad taking wheat to a grist mill once and bringing back about five hundred pounds of flour. It didn't cost cash as the mill kept the bran and midlings in exchange for the grinding.

Fuel was at a minimum as we had an unlimited supply of corn cobs for kindling and fast heat, and we had a goodly supply of fire wood most of the time on Maple Avenue. We did buy coal, but in the depth of The Depression, we could drive to the mines at Pekin and get it for as little as $1.25 a ton. We did buy anthracite coal (hard coal) for a much higher price since it was shipped in from Pennsylvania or West Virginia. During the coldest part of the winter, we used a "Base" Burner using hard coal that could be stoked in the evening and would burn all night, keeping the downstairs – at least the living room comfortable all night.

Consider with all this self-sufficiency, taxes were negligible. We had a small property tax – horses etc. but had no income tax or sales tax to pay. Our feed for the horses, the cattle, hogs, chickens was almost entirely raised on the farm, and all these animals reproduced without capital outlay. We did not buy fertilizer, herbicides or insecticides. The manure from the animals was spread and plowed under; we used a crop rotation of corn, oats, then legume hay to add nitrogen to the soil. Until hybrid corn came into use, we picked out the choice ears for seed, our own oats, and even our own clover and timothy for seed. Besides the corn and oats we sold, we had swine for marketing, five or ten gallons of Jersey cream each week, and sometimes eggs.

We had no house rent to pay; the house went with the farm, but we did have cash rent to pay on pasture and hay ground. That was seven dollars an acre down on Maple Avenue so that ran over three hundred dollars a year and took a sizable chunk out of the amount received from grain sales. We had to do all the planting, weeding, harvesting, delivery of the grain, and half the corn and oats went to Mr. Harrison, the landlord. From our share of the grain, after deducting the seed and the corn and oats fed to our animals, we would have no more than one thousand bushels of oats and about two thousand bushels of corn to market to pay the cash rent and other sundry expenses, both personal and farm.

We got by because we had no indebtedness to pay, no crop failures or other catastrophes. Power outages and electric bills were no problems to us in those days. Rural Electrification reached our farm in 1936. Our overhead was low indeed.

At any rate in 1932, the Bloomington Canning Company had gone broke and went out of business so three farms with a total of 800 acres they had rented from the David Davis estate became available. They had raised sweet corn and tomatoes on those eight hundred acres and had torn out all fences.

A Mr. McDermott was farm manager for Mrs. Lillard who I think was a daughter of David Davis — at least an heir. She owned over four thousand acres of land from his estate. McDermott offered Dad his choice of the three farms. Dad took the largest of the three- a half section, 320 acres. Davis land was much sought after by renters since they encouraged pasture and hay ground by charging only four dollars per acre cash rent and allowed the renter three fifth share of oat ground and still fifty percent of the corn crop. That farm was eighty acres more than we farmed on Maple Avenue.

This was all welcomed: lower rent, richer ground, more acreage, better share of small grain, but it was now 1932 and we were in the deepest part of The Depression. We had a good crop in 1932, more than fourteen thousand bushels of corn and probably four thousand bushels of oats and some soybeans, but during the corn harvest, corn prices dropped to twelve cents a bushel and oats were five cents. Had we sold our corn crop at that time, we would have grossed for our half, less than we could get some six years earlier with only two thousand bushels as our share. Actually we didn't sell then, but Dad did sell some corn for eighteen cents and later the rest of his share for something like twenty four cents. Pork was five cents a pound. We sold raw Jersey milk, testing six percent butterfat for twenty five cents a gallon. I delivered it on my way to school to customers along Suddith Road.

We still picked corn by hand, and Dad usually hired one man for corn husking since that season was during the school year. That year we had Orville and Clyde, two big strapping fellows who came up from Southern Illinois for the corn harvest. They rode the "rods" on the freight train to Bloomington and Dad offered them one cent, cash, per bushel of corn picked with another half cent per bushel when he sold the corn if the price went up to

The Great Depression

twenty cents. They wanted cash and compromised on one and a quarter cents per bushel. Of course we furnished board, lodging and laundry.

They with my brother Dean picked and husked more than fourteen thousand bushels between late September and early January. They were in the field before daylight with a lantern on the wagons; the three teams and wagons brought in an average of 110 bushels each day. After our crop was in, they picked some for George Cordiss, and when they caught the freight train for home at Bunker Hill, Orville the older brother had some $140 in greenbacks in his high boots. This could carry them through the rest of the winter until spring work opened up.

A few farmers who need hired help had tenant houses where they kept a man and wife. They furnished a cow for the couple to milk and a vegetable garden, and they could keep a few chickens. During the worst of The Depression, the monthly wages was the princely sum of twenty dollars. They did get by! Prices of everything were comparatively low. To go to the movies was ten or fifteen cents for children and twenty-five cents for adults; hamburgers were a nickel or at Bakers, six for a quarter. They weren't very big, but then lots of people couldn't go to movies or buy even a hamburger. I recall buying a pair of black and white sporty shoes. I think they only cost one dollar and ninety eight cents. They didn't fit well as they didn't have my size, but they were keen looking shoes so I squeaked along with them.

Things remained on the same tenor on the farm for about the next four years. The crops weren't quite so good in 1933, but the prices were a little better. 1934 was the big drought year with the Dust Bowl in the states farther West where they had no crops and no feed for their livestock. We came as close to having a crop failure as we ever had as the hot, dry winds of August shriveled the corn; then when corn was dying at the far north end of the farm, Dad found chinch bugs that had killed Stiver's wheat were streaming out of the wheat into our corn with millions of insects in weaving red streams.

We plowed a furrow around the infected corn, ran a creosote line on top of the furrow, and we dug postholes every thirty feet. The bugs would follow the creosote and most would fall in the holes. Every day it was my job to run the line, replenish the creosote where straw or other debris formed a bridge for the bugs and burn with kerosene post holes filled with bugs. A time or two we had to move the barrier father into the field, but we saved the crop with a loss of about fifteen acres. Our corn crop was thirty five bushels per acres, but that was good for 1934 and prices climbed.

The drought continued through 1935 and 1936, but we had crops. During the summer, especially in '34 and '36, temperatures went over one hundred day after day and many records were set. I shocked oats when the temperature was one hundred and fifteen degrees. We didn't work really long hours and took long noon hours as the horses' endurance was put to a test.

That year, 1936 - while the hot summer didn't make a lasting impression on me, the bitter cold winter did. I was in college and usually walked the two miles to and from school, but in the worst of the weather, my brother Dean drove me though we frequently had to put a team of horses to pull the Ford to get it started on sub-zero mornings. And our car was kept in a building. Besides that we had to scoop out the driveway to get to the road

The Great Depression

if the road had been opened. Snow fell, a real storm on Christmas day of 1935 and none melted until late March of '36. That snow, and many like it, piled up and my brother Dean and I scooped open the driveway morning and night as the wind kept blowing. We marveled at the number of times we scooped the same snow back and forth and wondered why we didn't wear it out.

A few times when blizzards closed up the roads, I took the street car to Bloomington and stayed with my Grandmother Rolofson who lived on East Jefferson. Sub zero temperatures were common, day after day, and we recorded on our own thermometer, records of twenty and twenty six degrees below zero. But nobody froze.

1937 was a congenial year. Crops were good and prices better and Dad bought the first new car he ever owned. It was a small cylinder Ford with six cylinders and the price was something like six hundred and twenty five dollars. He had purchased a new tractor a year or two earlier. I didn't drive the tractor much. I liked horses and used them while my younger brother Dale and Dean argued who would get to drive the tractor.

The Depression didn't really end until the Second World War began. On the farm things recovered somewhat with the Drought years as farm surpluses melted down, but wages and retail prices stayed low and unemployment stayed high. The New Deal programs didn't help all that much – most were welfare programs that made charity an honorable and accepted state. The War was the catalyst for recovery and prosperity. But in 1938 when I was graduated from Illinois State Normal University there were few jobs open. Porter Powell, a friend, went to work in a restaurant; Jack Hopkins finally got a teaching job in Arkansas that paid sixty dollars a month, and I was envied by some of my friends when I went to work immediately for the U.S. Weather Bureau for seventy five dollars a month.

Those who were wise and able enough to have physics, mathematics or music as their field fared better and usually got good positions. When I was a sophomore, my principal and coach at Wapella High School Lawrence Wade urged me to study science and math; but Monroe Melton, my superintendent at NCHS was a New Deal Roosevelt enthusiast and advised us seniors to go for the social sciences, economics, etc. Those were easy courses for me so I opted for social science, geography and physical education. I intended to teach but never got around to it. Fate has been kind to me even if my judgment has frequently been at fault.

My later experiences are dealt with to some degree elsewhere so least one might consider farm life of the 20's and 30's as a depressing, painful and unhappy period of life — let me say strongly — not so! If I suffered any privations, I was too dumb to notice. I had no acquaintances who were so affluent for me to be envious of them. Contentment was normal with me, and I had no regrets.

It would be difficult for a modern youth to consider life without television, radio, bicycles, scouting, programmed recreation, libraries readily available and vacation trips. It would seem inconceivable to add in homes without electricity, central heating, running water and similar amenities. But we did have employment. I had chores to do as far back as I can remember. By the time I was in fourth or fifth grade, I worked horses with harrows, rollers, corn cultivators. During the summer after my seventh grade, I went through the threshing run as a regular. Using the team of Dean and Slocum, I hauled oats and wheat to the elevators at Wapella, Birkbeck or Carls Springs.

Now threshing was a sort of recreation so I might mention some of my experiences. Before I was a "regular", I hauled some grain but mostly ran the water wagon. With a buggy and old Prince, I hauled several jugs with cool well water — we had no ice- in a constant round to all the men. I even got some small pay at times. That ended after sixth grade. Oats and wheat were cut and tied in bundles by the McCormick Reaper run by my Dad with a four horse team. My brother Dean and I did the "shocking".

We stood eight bundles upright with another on top to shed the rain. These shocks stood for a week or two to cure, and they were ready for threshing.

The threshing run was a community effort covering farms on both sides of the roads for six or seven miles with Maple Avenue in the center. Eighteen to twenty farms were included. Every farm furnished at least one man and team and those with large acreages more. We usually had sixty to eighty acres of small grain so Dad usually had to furnish three men. He pitched bundles; Dean ran a rack wagon and I the box wagon. To maintain parity and avoid arguments, everybody kept their turn throughout the usual three weeks of threshing. The first man to quit at night was the first up the next day. One year we would start at the east end of the run then the next year at the west end- thoroughly democratic. The housewives, where the crew was at noon, prepared the noon meal, and she and some of her friends had to start early to get ready for twenty five to thirty-five hungry men.

Of course there was horseplay. Walter Bishop was afraid of snakes so more than once he found either live or dead snakes in his jacket pocket. Dad abhorred mice so when Walter offered him a pipe fill from his Prince Albert can, Dad declined since he noticed tiny holes in the tin. Bert Moberly allowed he could stand a smoke and opened the tin to have a live mouse jump out into his lap. When we were threshing at Longbrakes, some of we boys found a nest of rotten eggs hidden away in the barn. We were nibbling away on some rather green apples when Bert Crum drove up to the thresher with a load of bundles. He was two or three years older than I, but I yelled, "Hey Bert, want an apple?"

"Sure," he answered so I let fly with an apple that he caught nicely.

"Here's another," I said and let fly with a rotten egg. He caught that nicely too. He couldn't leave the team to catch me, and I stayed alert and out of his reach the rest of the run.

Corn shelling was also a community project but in a slightly different way. This was usually accomplished in the dead of winter. Corn kept in the cribs for a long time, and farmers had extra time for this in the winter; prices were usually better then and in the dead of winter, the unpaved roads became hard roads with deep freezes, at least until past noon. It was done on a load for load basis. If Dad hauled two loads for Moberly then Bert would owe him two loads in return. This type of work exchange would carry over from year to year. I didn't get in on much of this as I was almost always in school at corn shelling time.

But here, again, there was rivalry. Dad always tried to be the first one to the sheller but had to race, especially with Burl Hickman and Cecil Covey. A lot of men and teams were involved as the sheller operator never intended to shut down waiting for wagons. On one bitter January day, Moberly was shelling, and Dad was up by 4 a.m., fed and curried his horses, had his usual big breakfast, left all the cows to be milked by his sons and hitched up to go. He heard a wagon rattling down the avenue, and he could beat it handily as we lived just across the road from Moberly's, but he heard another wagon tearing through the fields east of the Moberly's; he couldn't beat this one.

It happened that Covey who lived two miles east and a mile south was determined to be first that morning so he got started really early. He walked his horses until he got near Burl Hickman's then urged them to a fast trot, and when he passed Hickman's, Burl was harnessing his horses by lantern light. What he didn't know was that Burl had let the fences down and cut across the fields and was backing in to the sheller when he got there. Dad was second and Covey finished third. All were ahead of Moberly who lived there.

I still haven't said too much about recreation. Actually there was recreation in our work, especially when it was group or community work. The longest stretch of recreation was when school started. That I have mentioned elsewhere, but I always claimed my vacation began when school started. I have also mentioned that on Saturday work ceased at 4 p.m., for an evening in town – in Clinton. In my early years this meant a movie, mostly Westerns with Tom Mix, Hoot Gibson, Jack Hoxie, William Boyd. These were silent movies in my early years with a piano player keeping tempo with the action and a bass key banging when the fun fight was going on.

When all the country boys were in town, there was a bit of rivalry with the "townies" – mostly instigated by my cousin Roy. The only thing resembling a "rumble" was one Saturday night on the courthouse lawn. I bested my chosen opponent, as did Kelly Bishop, but we were the only ones to get in the fight. The rest stayed clear, especially my cousin Roy.

During the summer the Rolofson clan got together frequently for Sunday dinner and a day of frolic. We alternated Sundays between Uncle Monte's, Uncle Frank's, Uncle Bill's and our house. Our Grandparents Rolofson came down from Bloomington, and Grandmother Rolofson always brought numerous sacks of candy for her numerous grandchildren. Christmas was always at her house. She knitted many sweaters for her grandsons, and I got my first football and Daisy Air Rifle from her.

At an early age when we met on Sundays after seeing a movie at the K-Theater, our game was "cowboys and outlaws". Loren being the youngest, of the four boy cousins near my age, was designated the "bad" guy. In later years, Loren lamented about how on many a Sunday afternoon he spent most of the time locked in the cob house. He would be released just to be hunted down and locked up again.

Loren did get even with Roy one time. Grandmother Minnie Rolofson had given Daisy Air Rifles to the three oldest boys, Loren being too young. Loren kept begging Roy to let him shoot his gun. Roy wouldn't allow it saying he had no more BB's. As Roy lolled with his air rifle upright and one leg over the barrel, the way he had

The Great Depression

seen the frontiersmen do, Loren crept around behind and knowing Roy wasn't noted for truthfulness, pulled the trigger and shot Roy in the leg. It was a BB gun so no damage, except to Roy's ego.

The McCannon clan only got together once or twice a year. Of course Cousin Roy was always present to run things and get me in trouble since we were double cousins. His mother was a McCannon and my mother was a Rolofson. He got me in trouble when we got in Uncle Bill's watermelon patch; and while I bemoaned the fact we weren't in the same grade school, I'm sure I escaped scrapes as a result. Henry Short and Andy Wilson were his pawns at Heidelberg.

I mentioned the silent movies of my youth. The "talkies" arrived at Clinton in the late 20's and Technicolor shortly afterward. *The Gold Diggers of 1929* was the first movie I saw with both, and that was probably in 1930. "Tip Toe through the Tulips" and "Painting the Clouds with Sunshine" were songs introduced in that movie. Buster Keaton and Harold Lloyd and later W.C. Fields were my favorite comics. The first two with Charlie Chaplin belonged to the silent era as did Wheeler and Woosley.

We got our first Victrola (record player) with hundreds of records from our Chicago relatives when they got their first radio in the mid 20's. The first radio I heard was in 1927 when we went to a neighbors; the whole Avenue was there to hear the Dempsey-Tunney heavyweight fight.

Of course it was battery powered and pretty lousy reception. I think we got our first battery powered radio about 1930. We had two batteries and while one was in use, the other had to be carried to town to be charged up.

Stories For My Grandchildren

    My Grandfather Rolofson had a pool table stored away and gave it to us about 1928. Dad bought green felt and recovered it so the boys converged on our house frequently. I practiced incessantly, and it was rare that anybody beat me on my own table. Several years later around 1935, I wandered in to a pool hall in Bloomington, and a small time hustler inquired if I didn't want a game of 8 Ball. I agreed as the loser always paid and it only cost a nickel a game. He then suggested to make it interesting, we would play for a dime on the side. I had about a quarter in my pocket so as not to be a "cheapie", I said "Okay".

    He broke and cleaned the table. I didn't get a shot! I guess I must have had thirty cents because at that point I looked at the time and felt the fifteen cents I still had in my pocket and mentioned that it was later than I thought, and I would just have time for one more game. This time I broke, and I ran the table. I got my dime back, and he 'lowed it was just as well that we quit since we were too evenly matched. I never let on but that I was used to running the table frequently, and I don't think he had any more money than I did.

    I never objected when I got lucky to let others think I was more skillful than I was. Years later when I was in veterinary school, I worked for Bill Reiter as a carpenter. We were building a barn and this farmer had a horseshoe pit. Now I pitched horseshoes since I was a kid and ringers were not too infrequent for me, but one noon when Albert Fox asked me if I ever pitched horseshoes; quite naturally I said, "No, what's that?"

    Albert picked up the four shoes, explained how they should be thrown then let me try. I pitched the iron shoes – four ringers, one on top the other. I'm not sure I had ever done it before but this was something I couldn't pass up. I said, "Gee, I don't think I would be interested in this game. It seems too childish and easy." With that I sat down. Albert looked at Slim and Slim looked at Bob and none of them said a word, and not one of them ever challenged me to a game.

Illinois State Normal University

In glancing back over these pages, I see that I have rather glided over my years in going through college the first time. It wasn't that I had no memorable experiences there, but rather I guess I didn't take full advantages of the opportunity of higher education. This was in contrast to my second adventure into college, when with a family to consider, I couldn't afford to be lax or run a chance of failure.

My years at ISNU coincided with the Depression Years – 1934-1938.

ISNU was a state supported teachers college so cost was negligible. As I recall, it cost something like thirty-six dollars a semester. There was no tuition, and that cost included the library and textbook fee as well as all sports admission, school plays and all other special events. We lived about two miles away so I lived at home, walked to and from school most of the time and carried my own lunch.

I didn't flunk any course during the four years, but I can't say I distinguished myself either. I got A's in most geography courses, in both geology courses, a few in physical education and in economics. I received a number of B's and a great number of C's. The C's were predominately from education courses, and being a teacher's college, almost one third of our credits were in education. American Public Schools, High School Problems, Educational Psychology, Rural Sociology, Philosophy of Education and a large number of others were our lot. If you attended class and didn't fall asleep too often, you were likely to get a C. If you took some interest and read your assignments, you were still likely to get a C. The only course I really worried about was Philosophy of Education. That wasn't taken until our senior year, and if you didn't pass, you didn't graduate. It might have been the most boring of all, but I worked hard on it. It so happened the elderly lady who taught the class had to have an operation – an appendectomy- and scheduled it for the day school let out for Christmas vacation. She didn't want to miss any teaching.

When vacation was over, Buck Bishop and Chester Alexander, two fun loving characters, boasted that they were sure to pass Philosophy since they together spent fifteen cents for a get-well card to send to the teacher. They were a little nonplussed to find that I called on her in the hospital with a scrawny plant that cost me fifty cents. In my four years, that was my only B in an education course!

I did come awfully close to flunking Music Appreciation. Here again it was a one hour required course in your freshman year. I don't remember any exams, but one's grades depended on a music notebook wherein you took notes on music events you were supposed to attend. The high point of the season was a concert by the St. Louis Philharmonic Orchestra to be given at the school on a particular Thursday evening. That event was mandatory.

Now it also happened that the school required physical education courses. That particular term I elected to take boxing. I had boxed a bit with neighbors that had boxing gloves. Gene Hill taught the course and informed the freshman gym class that they were expected to enter the school intramural boxing tournament. That was fine with me as there wasn't anyone in the class near my weight (143 pounds) that could give me any serious problems. It was beside the point that there were a lot of upperclassmen entering the tournament with whom I had no experience.

Dusty Rhodes was one of those. He only weighed 142 pounds but was very tough and quick. He started to school at Wesleyan College on a football scholarship, but after breaking his collarbone and having to give up football, he lost his scholarship and transferred to ISNU. He was from "Little Egypt", the tough coal mining district of Southern Illinois. I watched him make short work of his first round opponent; then in the second fight he fought a really good sophomore by the name of Allen. It took two rounds to knock him out.

Meanwhile I got by my section easily enough but didn't knock my opponents out. At any rate the welterweight championship fight occurred on a Thursday evening after school. I have to rely on eyewitnesses because I had no memory of the match. My memory faded in the second round, and I am told he was awarded a TKO in the third when it became monotonous for me to get up off the mat. I crawled through the ropes, dressed and walked the two miles home.

I didn't do any chores that night or eat my supper. I went to bed and though my mother checked up several times on me, I slept until morning. I got out of bed that morning rather confused. Oh, I felt fine and looked in the mirror and saw no bruises or black eyes, but I did have a slight ache in my jaw. I had no memory of the bout. When I went down to breakfast and my mother found I was feeling well, she asked if I had a fight the previous evening. I asked her what day it was, and she answered Friday; I said I must have since it was scheduled for Thursday.

I guess I had "retrograde amnesia" from the knockout and still wasn't sure of anything until I got to school and found I had missed the St. Louis Symphony. Music Appreciation was the only D I ever got in college – and boy, did I ever have a good excuse!

Dusty never lost a match, at least in college, and won every fight by a knockout. Of course my boxing career record wasn't too bad if one merely mentions that I only lost one fight – and glide over the brevity of my boxing career.

English and literature courses will be mentioned because of one little bit of irony. Palmer, the head of the department, was my teacher my freshman year, and he was a stern grammarian. I wasn't too strong on grammar or on punctuation or any of the mechanics of this field, but I liked literature in all forms. In the spring of my senior year, I had all required credits and more hours than needed to graduate so I elected to take a two hour course in advanced writing. Palmer taught the course and announced that we would be turning in a composition of some sort on every class day which was Tuesday and Thursday afternoons. The next class period, Palmer would read some of the papers handed in- for comments, suggestions and criticism. Well, I liked to write and I had a bit of imagination; my compositions were read most of the time. I can still see Palmer chortling and sputtering as he read some of my compositions and saying, "Great stuff! Real Will Rogers vintage! Belongs in Creative Writing – not here!"

Then his humor would vanish and he would continue, "Oh, but the spelling, the punctuation, the paragraphing is deplorable!" When I would get my paper back, it would be covered by red marks and a big C in red at the top. It was a little disappointing to me, especially when some of my friends always begged for my papers and turned them in to Pop Cravens in another class and got an A. Of course they took heed of the red marks.

Well, the balmy days of spring came on, and Palmer decided this class was particularly unsound in grammar. He announced we would dispense with composition and devote the rest of the semester to fundamentals. This was of course a disappointment to me. Now by this time class attendance was optional and anyway I didn't need the course for graduation so I started my Thursday afternoon golf playing.

Jack Hopkins, a buddy of mine, had no classes on Thursday afternoon so he and I would check out golf clubs at the college gym, ride the streetcar to Highland Park where as students we could play eighteen holes for fifteen cents.

I didn't drop the class; I just went on Tuesdays. For six consecutive weeks we played golf on Thursday. I was sure, though it didn't worry me much, that I had flunked my first course. I don't know why, but that tough old boy Palmer gave me a C.

And now for the irony – so some would say "dumb luck". Eleven years later I had resigned my position with the CAA and was applying for admittance to veterinary school. Somewhere down in the fine print on requirements for entry – among chemistry, physics, biology, speech, animal husbandry and a pile of electives, was the requirement – "Two Hours Written Composition."

Palmer's gift of the C didn't embellish my grade point average, but it sure saved my neck.

Iowa City and George L. Stanton

Right off I want to state that George LaRue Stanton was one of my favorite people. He was also one of the most intelligent and capable persons with whom I worked. He, like all of us, had certain drawbacks; but certainly not among these drawbacks could be listed a lack of ability or intelligence. Neither could it be said that a sense of humor, generosity, imagination or originality was lacking. Actually George was a teeny bit lazy!

I first got to know George when we first entered college as freshmen. He was from the tiny village of Loami – not far from Springfield – a hamlet whose only call to fame was its being the home town of George's cousin Slim; also its euphonious name was mentioned in Vachel Lindsay's poem "The Santa Fe Trail." George was a high school athlete, but I could rarely ever get him interested in any physical activity after I got to know him. I think I got him out to play golf twice. Each time after several days nagging, and maybe one or two postponements, and then after I arranged the loan of a set of clubs and furnished golf balls and tees. The second and last time we went to the Finkbine course at Iowa City, and we made it around to what I believe was maybe the seventh hole. George had managed to lose two or three of my golf balls; since this was the lake hole, I hit around the north end of the lake and suggested firmly to George that he should do likewise. George informed me that he would have no difficulty driving over the pond and proceeded to deposit my ball in the middle of the lake. I put down another ball, mentioning the stark logic of my pathway to the green. There was another splash and George said, "See, that was much closer to the other bank, and all I have to do is hit it twenty five yards farther."

After the third splash, I said to George, "Look George, I only came out here with eight balls. Three you have lost in the rough and three you have put in this lake, but this is my last ball; I would hate to play in alone."

I think George really tried to go around this time, but he hit a big banana and my last ball went in! I would like to have reported that George may have evidenced some remorse, but he did offer some advice: "Buy more expensive balls and they will fly better."

Actually this discourse is about George Stanton and not about me although my first job was possible because of George and his influence. During our freshman and sophomore years we became good friends, but George failed to show up for our junior year. Some months later he wrote me and said he dropped out because he found a good job. It didn't pay much, but it didn't demand much work either – at least physical work. He was an Airways Observer with the US Weather Bureau.

You see this was in the Great Depression of the middle and later 30's when anyone with a job was envied, and if your employer was the US Government, it sounded much better than it was. In the spring of 1938, just before my graduation, I had been interviewed for a few teaching jobs. One job I tried for, but didn't get, paid nine hundred and sixty dollars a year. Another I could take but turned it down because it paid only $825 a year. I was a little discouraged, but then received a letter from George saying he had been transferred to Iowa City. He said there was to be an opening in June, and if I hadn't signed up, he would use his persuasive powers to get me the job. He said it didn't pay much but it sounded important; we would be working at the Iowa City airport, have fun and credit was easy for anyone with such an important sounding job.

I immediately applied for the job and received favorable response from Fred Flocken, the Operator in Charge. Flocken, in fact, said I was highly recommended and the job was mine except he needed my typing speed records. Our weather reports and flight traffic were transmitted by teletype and while I would have to learn the teletype and tape codes, that wouldn't take long for any good typist. I wrote back and reaffirmed my desire for the job but excused my omission of a typing speed since I hadn't gotten around to trying a typewriter. I added that I thought it was probably pretty good, and bound to improve, because I was going to start practice. I ended by saying, "By the way, what is the world record?"

George wrote back to say that I still had the job, as Flocken had told him that I indicated some confidence.

I was graduated on June 6, 1938 at 4 p.m., and Dad drove me to Iowa City that night for me to start work the next morning. I moved into an apartment with George and the third operator Bob Chamberlain. For two years the three of us lived together in the bachelor apartment and divided the twenty-four hour shifts at the Weather Bureau – with never a day off. Since I was the newest, I was stuck with the graveyard, midnight to 8 a.m., shift most of the time. Bob preferred the evening shift since his social life was simplified. His dates spent the evenings at the airport with him on duty and he never had to take them to movies etc. George was singularly adept at finding reasons for working the 8 a.m. - 4 p.m. shift.

This story was started just to describe the aviation career of Col. Stanton, although in 1938 and 1939 there was little to point to such a pursuit, as George was only lukewarm to the idea of flying. I, however, took to flying easily, and by getting bargain flying prices from Lain Guthrie, I soon had the minimum time logged and then soloed. I didn't have enough money to fly much, but in 1939 the government came up with the Civilian Pilot Training Program. Bob, George and I all enrolled. We all had different instructors and our flying time didn't interrupt our work time, but we had to fix a schedule of work so that each of us missed ground school (navigation, meteorology, air regulations) taught at the University of Iowa every third day. After the minimum of thirty five flying hours, we all passed the flying exams and the written examinations to get our private pilot's license. That was it for Bob and me, but George found he could sign up for secondary or acrobatic flying at 7 a.m. This would mean he would have to have the day shift so he signed up.

After secondary flying, they then offered a cross-country course which was almost always night flying so of course George signed up for that too so he could stay on that day shift. Before the cross country course had been completed both Bob and I were married, and I had moved to Montezuma, Iowa as an Airways Communicator with the Civil Aeronautics Administration.

Our weather bureau job was not Civil Service and pretty much a blind end. However in 1939 a Civil Service Examination was given for the CAA job, and of course Bob, George and I all took it. I don't know how it happened, but I beat George on this examination. He only missed two questions on the exam, but I didn't miss any. Because of my one hundred percent, I was offered a job right away, and George also some four months later was offered the same job at Anthony, Kansas. By the time George was offered his job, his cross country flying course was completed, and most of his fellow flyers were eagerly trying to enlist in the Air Corps. George had the best record but was dubious about flying since he thought we were drifting toward war. He wasn't enthusiastic about our preparedness so he came over to Montezuma to talk to me. I convinced him that not only was the CAA his type of job, but chances for advancement was good as the CAA was expanding its communication network and facilities.

When George left me, he was all set to accept the CAA job and pass up the Air Corps. Now George by this time owned an automobile, and his fellow flying students talked him into driving them to Des Moines so they could try to enlist. This was before Pearl Harbor, and the Air Corps was still very choosy about who they accepted. One boy was rejected because he was an inch too short and others rejected on the basis of their ground school marks or skill; but George, who had no intention of enlisting was the one they wanted. It so happened that the group had paused at more than one tavern between Iowa City and Des Moines so that when they returned, only one had been picked outright; that was George.

The Air Corps sent Stanton to Corciciana, Texas for primary training and though cadets were washed out right and left, George sailed through with top marks for both skill and ground school. He then went through Briggs Field and was selected for Randolph Field, the West Point of the air. A good number of the newly graduated flyers were sent to Hawaii or the Philippines. Most were shot down or captured early in the invasion without even flying one combat mission, but not George. His record was such that they kept him in Texas to give instruction to the flood of cadets they were now admitting. He never left Texas during the Second World War.

When the war ended, George wanted out because they had him on instruction of our international allies. He was teaching the Nationalist Chinese, the Turks, and the Koreans at Enid, Oklahoma. He came up to see me at Chanute, Kansas and explained how since he could only communicate to his students through an interpreter, he figured he took his life in his hands every time he went up with them. He wanted me to see if I could help get him into the CAA. He explained that his brother could get him a job with Caterpillar Tractor Company, but that would be unsatisfactory since they indicated a certain amount of work was expected.

I contacted our District Office at Kansas City and went with George to see our top personnel there. Yes indeed, they wanted George who was now a Captain or Major, but it would take a little maneuvering. Congress had provided re-employing of all former government employees who were in the service, but unfortunately George, who at one time accepted the CAA job at Anthony, never reported so he was never employed. We brought up the matter of his Weather Bureau job so they called the Weather Bureau and while the Weather Bureau didn't need any more employees, they agreed to restore him- provided the CAA would ask for his transfer immediately. I went home sure that George and I would once again be serving at the same station.

    The next time I got a letter from George, he had reenlisted. It seemed that the lowly job we once held at Iowa City not only no longer existed, but it was unclassified and therefore there were no reemployment rights. Rather than go to work, he decided to put up with his uncommunicative clientele at Enid.

    I sort of lost track of George for a while until his next enlistment came up. It seemed that after some ten years, someone discovered the Major Stanton had never had combat duty or even a hardship assignment. By this time, I had left the CAA and was back in college at Manhattan, Kansas when George came to see me again. It was obvious, since we were no longer at war, the combat duty couldn't be met; George couldn't convince them that San Antonio and Enid were hardship assignments so they decided to send him to Fairbanks, Alaska.

    George came to see me because he wanted a security check and a recommendation. You see it was discovered that George had never finished college either so he had placed an application for the Air Corps to send him back to school for his degree. The same mail that directed him to report to Fairbanks also carried his acceptance into Boston University. George completed his two remaining

Iowa City and George L. Stanton

college years in one calendar year and was graduated cum laude. This so impressed his superiors that they decided to send him back to college for his Masters Degree.

After receiving his Masters Degree, George became a Colonel and finished his military career as personnel director for the Northeast Air Command. Not bad for a lad who wasn't that crazy about flying; who had too many beers enroute to Des Moines.

The last time I saw George he was back where he started. Retired from the military and doing personnel work for the state government at Springfield, Illinois.

George and the Gold-Plated Dresser Set

So far I have rather outlined Stanton's military career but largely ignored the two and a half years of our carefree bachelor years at Iowa City. It was a good period. We had little money, no autos and looked forward to the one time each month when we got our pay checks. We all had the same salary so upon receipt of our checks, each of us- Bob, George and I- coughed up ten dollars to pay our rent and split the cost of our grocery bill we ran up at the corner grocery. In addition, George usually had borrowed a couple of dollars from Bob or me – each time saying, "Mac, I'll never beat you out of this loan. I may owe you the rest of my life, but I'll never beat you out of it."

He always ran short a week before payday as we all usually did, but he believed in postponing payment for a couple of days as he claimed he liked to carry a few bucks to feel prosperous, if only for a day or two.

It was in December of 1939 when George and I went to Cedar Rapids to do some shopping for Christmas. I was looking for a gift for the girl who was to become my wife, and George had plenty of suggestions. He, on the other hand, had three girls to buy for. There was a local

George and the Gold-Plated Dresser Set

blonde and another blonde he had some dates with while in college and with whom he kept corresponding; but his main object was Florence, a brunette from his home town who was in school at the University of Illinois.

George liked to shop; he liked to haggle and he wasn't averse to buying. We finished at a jewelry store which featured quite a selection of dresser sets. They ranged in price from fifteen dollars up to fifty eight dollars for one gold-backed set that even had a clock. The proprietor, sizing us up right away, extolled the virtues of the sets in the medium price range of around twenty-five dollars. Because of his overstocking, he generously dropped down to twenty dollars. You have to remember that this was 1939, the later stages of The Great Depression, and we were making only from seventy- five dollars to eighty dollars a month. When George continued his haggling, we finally got to the rock bottom price of eighteen dollars, and I bought and paid for a nice blue set. At this point George began dickering for the gold- backed set. He got the price down to fifty dollars; we made starts to leave then wandered back for one more look, with the proprietor dropping the price about a dollar on each return. At the door I would try to convince George he couldn't afford the set, and he would explain how much it had lowered in price, and after all that was real gold.

Somewhere around forty-four dollars George agreed to buy the set. The proprietor was relieved, but immediately perplexed when George advised he would be forced to pay for it on time. After all I paid cash for mine. George finally convinced him that he had a good job with the U.S. Weather Bureau, but being momentarily at low ebb, he could only pay five dollars down. When the proprietor finally got the terms and documents ready, George turned to me and said, "Mac, lend me five dollars."

That wasn't quite the end of the dresser set story. John Harvey was a friend from the Springfield area who worked at construction part of the time, but when he was laid off, he would come to Iowa City for an extended visit. He came in December and as he was returning home for Christmas, George trusted the dresser set to him to deliver to Florence. John claimed it was too good and he just might give it to his girl friend. He delivered it, but almost didn't when he found that Florence had become engaged at Christmas to a college student. In the many months George was making payments on that dresser set, I never once alluded to that purchase.

A year or two later, when I was with the CAA and George was graduating from Randolph Field, I did mention it. You see the college engagement fell through, and George and Florence were married when George got his commission on graduating from Randolph. Upon receiving the announcement, I wrote George a long letter of congratulations and told him that I knew that somehow, sometime he would get back that gold-plated dresser set.

The U.S. Weather Bureau

Solo Feb 15, 1939

The U.S. Weather Bureau

My two and a half years with the Weather Bureau coincided with my years at Iowa City. Both began in June, 1938 upon my graduation from I.S.N.U. As mentioned elsewhere, though the job sounded important, the pay was undoubtedly the lowest in the entire government service of the USA—and much of my experiences during that time are mentioned in the Saga of George Stanton.

The title of our jobs was "Airways Observer" and was primarily that of taking weather readings and transmitting them by teletype over the weather circuits throughout the United States and Canada. We were of course stationed at the Municipal Airport and handled flight plans, aircraft accidents information, as well as furnishing weather information, all by teletype, to United Airlines stationed there.

Now because we were the Weather Office, people called in for forecasts and weather information, though we weren't the designated official forecasters. There were no rules prohibiting us from doing private forecasting; though when radio stations or the newspapers called, we just relayed the official forecasts.

George and I bewailed the generalization of forecasts and the terms "possible showers", "probable snow", or "strong winds" became more exact when it was for someone we knew or for local consumption not likely to come to the attention of the Big-Wheels in the Bureau. George got a big kick out of assisting housewives when they called to advise them whether or not they should allow the furnace to go out at night or whether to plan on the next day for family washing. He didn't hedge; he gave them positive answers, though we never knew whether it always turned out as he assured them.

There were a couple of times that stick in my memory on my positive prognostications. One Sunday afternoon we had had a couple of thundershowers pass through, though I knew a severe turbulent storm had just passed Cheyenne and would reach Iowa at night. The evening was clear and balmy when a couple of patrolmen stopped in as they frequently did. Hamm was night captain and Ryan was his buddy. Hamm said, "Well, Mac me boy, she's a lovely night since the storms passed."

"It's not over," I said. "We've got one more to hit us tonight, and it is a lulu, lots more wind, and lightning with this one."

"Oh," said Hamm, "and when is this lulu going to show up?"

"It's going to hit here at exactly 10:27 P.M.," I replied. We were "exact forecasting" right at that time.

Both Hamm and Ryan chuckled when they left and headed for the station. There someone commented on the weather being so fine, and of course Hamm warned them it wasn't over, and that we were going to have a nasty one at exactly 10:27 that night. In taking the bus home, when the driver or someone he knew brought up the subject of weather, Hamm of course warned them to look out for a bad one at 10:27.

Hamm retired early that night and promptly fell asleep. He was awakened by a loud clap of thunder. Lightning was flashing, the wind howled, and rain was pouring down. His wife was up and busily shutting down the windows. Hamm sat bolt upright and said, "Honey, what time is it?"

"Ten thirty," she answered. "And what are you laughing about?"

The other memorable forecast I would mention involved Paul Shaw. Paul was one of the two pilots scratching a living out of flying there at Iowa City. He had an ancient Buell four seater, and while he did give some flight instruction, his main income was taking a few fares up for a flight over Iowa City on beautiful evenings. There were two hangars at the airport. One housed the few small planes there and the other had tall sliding doors on both sides that were opened twice a day for the two United flights that stopped at Iowa City. United used Boeing 210, I believe they were called—not large planes, two engines, pilot, co-pilot and a stewardess. They only carried ten passengers or so.

You see this was 1938 so on balmy summer evenings many citizens of this small city turned out to see these planes land, taxi into the hangar, while the smartly clad United personnel pushed up the unloading platform, tended to any passengers getting on or off, refueled, then the plane engines would grind to a roar, taxi on through and take off for Chicago or Omaha.

United owned both hangars, and Paul worked off his hangar rent by trimming hedge and grass. Lain Guthrie (whose place I took as Airways Observer) had two Piper

The U.S. Weather Bureau

Cubs, and gave most of the flying instruction. He didn't own a car but had two planes so he rented the entire second hangar. He didn't have grass to cut so Paul wouldn't use his hangar space and usually tied his plane outside, but on stormy nights he would wait until the last United flight came in at 10:10 P.M., then before the doors were pulled shut would push his plane in the other hangar for the night.

The first week I was at Iowa City I had to file my first accident report. It was of course on Paul Shaw. When I arrived, Paul had his right arm in a cast—having gotten it tangled in the prop of his Buell while starting it. That didn't stop his flying; so one evening when I was on duty, Paul took a young man and his date up for a flight. Before he cleared the airfield, the motor on the Buell conked out and he came down in an oat field at the end of the runway. The landing was OK but the oats wrapped up the landing gear and stood the Buell on its nose, breaking the prop and damaging the cowling. No one was injured, not even Paul's arm in the cast. But I had to file my first accident report.

Paul couldn't afford to fix up the old Buell, so he eventually traded it for an older Welch, a squat ground-hugging mongrel that could fly but hated to leave the ground. He flew it through a fence or two when it refused to leave the ground, and eventually traded it for a Taylor craft. That was a pretty good small plane, and it was the one he had on the night I was leading up to.

Shaw was an "Old-timer' and began flying near the end of the First World War. He had numerous small mishaps, but never one he couldn't walk away from. A year or two later after the time I am describing, he asked me if I wanted to fly his new Taylor Craft 65 Hp to

Burlington. We were having a minor air show at Iowa City, and we were going to obtain the showing of an antique 1912 canvas and piano-wire plane. Of course it couldn't fly from Burlington to Iowa City, so had to be trucked up. On the day of the show, it flew from one end of the runway to the other end.

At any rate, as we flew south (I never turned down a free plane ride), he would reminisce. "See that pasture down there? That's where I flew the Welch through the fence." And later, "That oat field down there, that's where I cracked up the Old Flying Jenny." I was doing the flying and our present plane was a new one, but I certainly got the impression that many a field was the scene of one of Paul's minor mishaps.

Well, back to the event I was telling about. It was a Sunday evening in summer—balmy and pleasant. Shaw's Taylor Craft was tied just west of the Weather Bureau building, and the parking lot was full of cars whose owners were enjoying the pleasant evening and were there to see United land and take off.

Paul had called me to inquire if dangerous weather was in the offing, or if he could forget about his plane. I was watching a cold-front that was marching across Nebraska with some hail and wind gusts up to 45 mph. He then inquired if it would hold off until after the last United flight had taken off. I told him it would be a close race, but if United was on time, it would hold off, but just barely.

Shaw came out, but the weather was still pleasant when United landed a minute or two before its scheduled time of 10:05 P.M., and he leaned on the fence chatting with people he knew. I went out and told him the storm had passed Des Moines quite some time earlier.

Lightning was continuous in the west when United took off, so I again went out and said the storm has passed Montezuma. He still lingered until the United people started closing the doors. When he began untying his plane, I rushed out to help just as the first crashes of thunder sounded and he became hurried for the first time. We started pushing the plane to the hangar which was only about a hundred feet away. We hadn't gone more than forty feet when the howling wind hit us. He was on the tail and I was on the windward wing, and for a while we held our own, but the wind increased; the tail whipped and slammed Paul into the fence. The plane then took off. I bailed out about six feet off the ground, and the plane sailed over the weather building, came down on a couple of cars and cart wheeled into two others, upside down. We went into the Weather Bureau Building, which wasn't touched by the plane. Paul sat for about forty-five seconds with his head in his hands then said, "Well, let's go out and see how many people we killed."

There were no injuries. The cars that the plane landed on were steel topped and caved in, but with the storm, everyone went for shelter and when the plane hit, people saw it coming and lay down in the seats.

I had another accident report to file.

As I said earlier, newspapers and others got their official forecasts from Des Moines, but they did frequently call up to get our official current readings. Usually they were factual, but we sometimes embellished the facts. I recall one January day when the weather could scarcely be worse. The temperature was somewhere near zero; the sky and visibility were zero, and we had a sizable snowfall earlier. It was still snowing, but you couldn't tell it because the wind was in the northwest blowing about 35 mph with stronger gusts, and both ground and falling snow was moving horizontally in a blinding mass.

Now I will pause and describe our weather building. It was a small, one room shack that once housed the field flood lights. There was a window and door on both the east and west sides and the building could scarcely be heated. We had an oil burner that gave off some heat, but not much more than that generated by the electric teletype machines. One night I came on at midnight, and Bob Chamberlain had his heavy coat, cap, and gloves on, and was sitting on the stove. Water froze at the north end of the building indoors. Only one time can I remember it being too hot in winter. Fred Flocken, the boss, decided the heat was all going up the chimney, so had gotten extra pipe and elbows and ran a big rectangle of stove pipe around the room before it exited through the roof. That worked for a few days, then when enough oily soot settled in the horizontal stove pipe, it became ignited and we had red hot stove pipe scorching the ceiling. Water had to be thrown on the pipes before the building burned.

Well, we put up with the colder room thereafter. In addition, the doors were indoor doors and in the summer with higher humidity, they swelled until they couldn't be closed. Flocken would use his plane and shave the doors until they could be closed. Of course, when winter came, the wood of the doors shrank, leaving rather sizable spaces around.

Now on this particular January day, a reporter from the *Press Citizen* called. He wanted to know how the weather was out there. "How fast is the wind?"

I answered, "You mean indoors, or out?"

He chuckled and asked, "You mean you can feel it inside?"

"Well," I said, "we don't have an anemometer indoors, but our Venetian blinds are standing straight out." I went on further. "Gusts are hitting up to forty-five mph outside, but I doubt if they are more than twenty-five inside."

"If it's that bad out there," he continued, "you may feel a little snow inside."

"Well, it's not too bad," I said. "It's only about six inches deep inside."

"How long will it be before your room fills completely?" he asked.

"Oh, it won't get any deeper," I answered. "It's blowing in the west side, but it's blowing back out through the cracks on the east side."

He appreciated the story and said he would file the report with United Press.

He called later to apologize to me when the story went out. After being modified by a couple of editors who thought their job was to make their reporting believable, they rather cobbled up what I thought was a good job of weather reporting.

University of Iowa Summer School

I intended to qualify as a meteorologist since I had taken courses in both meteorology and climatology at INSU. Unfortunately all the big wheels in the Weather Bureau were physics teachers or physics majors, so when Civil Service Exams were given, all applicants were required to pass the physics part before the math and meteorology parts were graded. To prepare for this, I enrolled at the University of Iowa to take a summer course in beginning physics. That didn't work out. The exam was given before the summer course was well underway, and my physics instructor didn't help me any. It was supposed to be beginning physics, but he went about it as though we were all physics majors and had one or two years already under our belts.

He never really worked out a problem to conclusion, and delighted in using symbols and Greek letters to display a mystifying web of symbols, and would then say, "Now you can see the equation, so we won't work it out farther."

When someone said they didn't understand, he would brush it off with, "Well, you just work on it. We won't take class time on anything this simple."

On one occasion, he had a problem of a streetcar weighing so much, and of people of a certain weight mounting on the rear end which was a certain distance back of the rear wheels, and how many could get on that part before the streetcar tipped up. Well, he filled the blackboard several times with gibberish and couldn't solve it. I volunteered to solve the problem, but he brushed my solution off as childish, even after one student volunteered that my answer was correct as he had looked up the answer.

Well, the professor couldn't work the problem, so he put it off until the next class, then came back and showed his usual hieroglyphics, saying, "This is how you do this. McCannon had a way, but it wasn't the proper way to go at it."

A few days later, this professor gave us a leverage problem. A foot ruler weighing a certain number of grams protruded over the edge of a desk by some five and one half inches. A fly weighing a given number of milligrams walked out on the ruler. The problem was how far could the fly walk before it tipped the ruler off the desk. I think I could have worked it out given a lot of time, but he wanted an instant answer. No one in class had the faintest idea of how to go about solving the problem. He rather sneeringly said, "You mean that in this physics class there's nobody that can even present an idea as to how to go about solving this problem?"

Of course I volunteered. I had already decided I wasn't learning anything and had decided to drop the class so I said, "Well, place the ruler in position, catch a fly, pull off its wings, dip its feet in red ink and chase it out on the ruler. Where the footprints leave off – there you have the answer!"

The class enjoyed my solution. The professor didn't smile; he looked rather pityingly in my direction and went on to another subject. I didn't show up after that. My tuition wasn't entirely wasted. I was able to use the gym facilities at the university, play the Finkbine Golf Course for something like twenty-five cents a round and otherwise had the same privileges as any other summer school student.

I believe it was the following summer I had the same privileges. The government began the Civilian Pilot Training Program and Chamberlain, Stanton and I all entered. Ground school (navigation, meteorology, airway regulations and communication) was conducted by the engineering department of the university. Of course Bob, George and I took turns at missing class since one of us had to be on duty at all times, but we had no problems. All the classes got along well except in meteorology, and it was taught by a member of the physics department. Shortly before the final exam was given, Dr. Lundquist (head of the program) who taught navigation came in and gave us exams on all subjects. It was an exam the government had given previously. There were thirty in the class (three women) and of those thirty, twenty-six flunked. Of the four that passed, three of us worked for the Weather Bureau. Well, Lundquist taught the rest of the term just what we had to know in meteorology so I think the rest of the class on the final passed everything.

On one particularly hot summer afternoon, as the physics teacher was droning on in meteorology and writing endless formulas and equations of the blackboard, the girl sitting next to me – we were seated alphabetically (her name was Montgomery) whispered, "If I don't get out of here, I'm going to fall asleep."

I whispered back, "I'm not too sleepy, but I'd far rather be out at Finkbine playing golf."

University of Iowa Summer School

"So would I," she answered.

The door to the room was open, and we were only a few steps away so I said, "The next time he turns to the blackboard, slip out and I'll follow."

By golly she did and I did and we had an afternoon of golf. The teacher never missed us although the class woke up when we slipped out. The buzzing caused the professor to look around, but he didn't know we left. I never asked Montgomery to play golf again. She was too good. I think she beat me.

As mentioned before, being enrolled at the university allowed you certain privileges. One event was an occasional dance, I believe held at the gym or field house. It was supposedly a "get-acquainted" event. Since quite a number of the summer students were female teachers back to continue their educational studies, I attended a couple. Now, I most assuredly wouldn't try to pass myself off as a ballroom artist. I didn't really dig or care for that sport, but it was a good way to meet a number of summer chicks. Back at Normal Community I signed up for dancing, and I think one session was all I was able to attend since it interfered with football practice.

There were those who considered that even with one practice session, I should have developed some skill other than giving the impression of a football skirmish. Anyway, that's how I met Olive Gardner. She was teaching at Greeley and spent a couple of summers at Iowa City. I always thought she considered that I might have had some sterling character since ballroom dancing definitely wasn't among such skills. We had a number of dates, but it was no surprise that she never insisted on going to dances.

Besides a few movies, we several times went out to a pub at Coralville where you could obtain a large and pretty good steak with French fries and salad for the big sum of thirty-five cents. When she took me home to meet her parents and then to Chicago to visit her sister, the realization arrived that we were going "steady", and my bachelor days were nearing an end.

1928 Nash

Arabella

The second summer I experienced three significant events. I acquired my first car Arabella, I passed the Civil Service Exam for the CAA and when summer ended, on the 28th day of September, Olive and I were married.

My Uncle Hugh Rolofson, while in the army in the First World War, was stationed at Waco, Texas as a mechanic working on the early aircraft of that time. Later he was with the Nash Garage in Bloomington and usually had good cars. Arabella was a Nash convertible – tan and gold- and had a rumble seat. Now I say convertible but I think I only took the top down once and had so much trouble getting it back that part of the description was dropped. It was something like ten or eleven years old when Uncle Hugh sold it to me for seventy five dollars. If I still had it now, it would be a real vintage car. It was a 1928 model.

Before Arabella and I met, I had to hitch-hike or borrow Bob Chamberlain's car to make the sixty or seventy mile trip to Greeley to call on Olive. That wasn't easy as I, like Bob and George, had to put in eight hours at the airport daily, seven days a week. We worked it out by taking the midnight shift then be off until 4 p.m. the next day. That didn't leave much time for sleep, but at ages twenty or twenty-five you don't need much sleep. At any rate I didn't see Olive too frequently except in the summer.

After Arabella, and with Olive teaching at Jessup, the trip was easier but I will relate one winter trip. I left Jessup about 1 a.m. with a light snow falling all the way to Independence. Turning south the snow changed to freezing rain and the road became an ice rink. Just as bad, I couldn't see out the windshield. The hand operated wiper couldn't help and when I stopped and cleaned off the ice, it would be glazed over before I could get back in so I had to drive with the left window down and my head mostly outside. Later I caught up with another car and could pull in my head and let my ears thaw as I could see his headlights through the iced over windshield. That worked for a while as we Cadillaced along about fifteen mph. That person evidently tired of leading me and turned off and stopped. After I passed him, he pulled in behind and followed me. That only lasted a few miles as I saw him pull right and leave me. About that time I discovered that I was no longer on

Arabella

highway 150. I was on a gravel road going somewhere but not toward Iowa City. I think I backed out all the way to the highway and eventually caught up with my lead car again. That didn't last long as he turned off at the next little town. He either lived there or gave up traveling farther. From there on, I was on my own.

I got through Cedar Rapids easily as street lights and a complete absence of autos made the going easier. The twenty miles between Cedar Rapids and Iowa City was the worst part of the trip. Arabella, however, performed beautifully. Going down a hill I would push her to the limit then let her momentum carry us over the next rise. You couldn't accelerate uphill as that would whirl her around. We did fine until we came to the steepest hill at the Iowa River. We got up a real head of steam going downhill and made it up more than three-fourth of the way to the top of the next hill before she stalled out. The right wheels were in the "run-off" gutter and I could keep her steady by keeping her in gear at low speed with the wheels slowly turning over. I tried to set the brakes but she started sliding down the hill. I could keep my position only by keeping the engine turning over slowly and the tires wearing out the ice underneath. I couldn't move ahead and didn't dare slide back down.

Finally, I did what I had to do. I left Arabella in gear with the wheels turning over slowly and walked down the hill where the highway department had filled a barrel with sand for just such emergencies. I don't know what container I had; it might have been my hat, but it wouldn't carry more than a half-gallon of sand. After three or four trips up and down, I got enough and spread thinly on the ice for Arabella to claw her way to the top. I knew we couldn't make it all the way as I lived at number three Triangle Place up a steep slope. We did get to the city limits. There a long slope, nowhere near the steepness of the river hill, stretching a quarter of a mile. Halfway up, Arabella was finished. I got her off the road and walked home. I went after her the next day after the streets were sanded. I shouldn't say the next day; it was the same day as it was after 4:30 a.m. when I got to the city limits.

Prospects were a little better in the summer of 1940. I still was making the same money, but after taking the Civil Service exam and making a hundred percent, I was listed twenty-fifth in line for a CAA job- for the whole country. The reason that I wasn't listed better was that my typing speed was only up to forty five words per minute, and there were many veterans who got a five percent bonus added to their grades.

So on September 27, Olive came to Iowa City when school was over and the next day when I got off work at 8 a.m., Olive, Arabella and I headed for Missouri. We heard that anyone with two dollars for a license and a willing partner could get instantly spliced. That we did at Palmyra, Missouri and made it to Keokuk, Iowa for a Saturday one day honeymoon then back to Jessup and Iowa City the next day.

Now the reason for a Missouri marriage was twofold. It was quick. Get a license at the county courthouse and find a Presbyterian minister who could spare a few minutes and it was over and as permanent as one with a week of festivities. More importantly, news of the union was not likely to drift back to Iowa. At that date female teachers were expected to remain single. I don't know how that state of affairs affected their teaching abilities, but to keep her job she couldn't divulge her new title. We

Arabella

couldn't afford that as she was making more money than I was. She continued on at Jessup and I at Iowa City. I guess she wore her engagement ring but not the wedding band except when I came up. And that wasn't too frequently.

The Civil Aeronautics Administration

I received my notice of appointment to the CAA and was to report to Montezuma, Iowa on January 15, 1941. Montezuma was about fifty miles west of Iowa City and a much smaller county seat town. The work was much the same except that I no longer had to work every day, got thirty dollars a month more and radio transmission, sending and receiving, was added.

When Olive's school was out, she too moved to Montezuma. She had acquired a few items for the household and we purchased a gas stove and a Kelvinator – on time- and I had rented half of a duplex so we were in business. Rent was twenty five dollars a month so we barely got by. Of course we ran with the Country Club set which included about everyone who wasn't on welfare. I remember our Country Club dues were twenty dollars a year and that included golf. We managed to scrape up the dues. The golf course was nine holes – sand greens, but it was golf.

I guess I did well at Montezuma. We lived there a year and I got top grades on tests given by the inspectors when they came around – that is everything except teletype speed. The second inspection I gave the inspector my personnel rating form and it was adopted

The Civil Aeronautics Administration

and used for a couple of years in the seven states making up the Fifth District.

I'm afraid I was the boss's favorite. Cedric Barnes was the man in charge there and when he left to transfer to Spearfish, South Dakota, he tried to get me transferred with him. That wasn't allowed as you had to work a year before you could be promoted or transferred. Ced was a real fine and intelligent individual, an engineer and graduate of Grinnell. He was also a friend of and schoolmate of Harry Hopkins of Roosevelt's Cabinet. Ced liked good books, good music and was a real leader and at times a trouble-shooter for the CAA. He wasn't ambitious and had no intention of clawing his way upward in the organization. He ran a tight ship but wouldn't accept a promotion if it meant mixing in with the rat-race in a bigger station or larger city.

We had personnel changes as the CAA was expanding as we approached the time of the Second World War. Sam Jones had about five to seven years in our grade and was finally promoted. Bryant then came and was a very capable operator, but the second newcomer was something else. His name was Lunch. I have no memory of a first name and though I'm sure he had one, he was just called Lunch; although, around town they referred to him as "The Blue Plate Special".

Lunch was of Russian extraction and came from Washington, D.C. The only work he ever had was as stenographer. I guess that's how he qualified for the job as he could type at blinding speed — more than ninety words a minute.

When Lunch was notified he had an appointment at Montezuma, Iowa, he was a bit concerned as to where he was going. He had never been away from the immediate area around Washington. He had heard of Iowa and was aware that it was somewhere in the Midwest. He also had heard of St. Louis and knew it was also in the Midwest so he took a bus and arrived at St. Louis. He was chagrined to find that he was nowhere near Montezuma and still wasn't in the right state. Since Des Moines was a good sized town and in Iowa, he took another bus to Des Moines; he was of the impression that Montezuma was one of the suburbs.

Arriving at Des Moines he found that there were still fifty miles of cornfields between him and his destination and furthermore, there were no buses, trolleys or other public transportation to Montezuma. He had never owned or needed an automobile in Washington but now realized there was a lot of space in the Midwest and little alternative to automotive transportation.

Lunch still had thirty dollars or so in his pocket so he visited a used car lot. Well, the honest citizen there, after finding how much money Lunch had, sold him an old Ford for twenty-five dollars and even got it started and pointed Lunch eastward toward Montezuma. The Ford was evidentially a city car and didn't choose to leave town and went dead at the city limits. Lunch knew nothing about cars, or he wouldn't have gotten stuck with this one, so he put in a call to the CAA station. Ced found out where Lunch was stuck and told him he knew a few things about cars and would drive over and get him going.

Well, Cedric found trouble in the ignition and cobbled it up and got the car started again. When he listened and heard the pistons slapping around, he knew the life of the car wasn't far from over so he told Lunch to drive modestly and he would follow. Well, the old car

The Civil Aeronautics Administration

gasped along for about twenty miles and was then finished. Cedric said later he didn't try any more so he told Lunch he had a rope in his car and he would pull him in behind his Whippet.

Five miles from Montezuma Ced felt a jerk and knew a tire had blown on the Ford but he didn't stop. He knew that Lunch wouldn't have thought to ask the salesman if there was a spare tire, and of course, there wasn't any. Lunch tried to sound the horn but of course it didn't function either so he stuck his head out and yelled, but Ced didn't look around and kept on going.

That was Lunch's triumphal entry into Montezuma. He pulled up to the only boarding house in town with a dead car pulled by a Whippet, on three tires and no horn. When Ced got out, Lunch said, "Hey, I blew a tire way back there. Didn't you hear me yelling?"

Ced's reply was, "Huh? What did you say? I'm a little bit deaf you know."

Well, the Ford sat there on the street until Lunch got a little money from home and he traded the old junker plus some cash in for another old loser. It was a bigger car, a Chrysler or Lincoln but only slightly better. Lunch could get it started but it overheated after only a few miles and wouldn't start again until it got cooled down. He thought he had a great car and explained to me (while he stared at my Arabella) that he was used to large automobiles and just didn't dig the little ones. Since the airport where the CAA station was located was just three miles out of town, the big car seemed fine. Then one day he started to Oskaloosa some twenty miles away. Well, he never got there. It would drive five miles – sleep for an hour – drive five miles – again take a nap. He was gone most of the day before he finally got back to town.

Lunch didn't have any more luck with the CAA than what he had with his automobiles; he never got to the place where we could trust him on watch on his own, and he came to the realization that he didn't belong in the Midwest. He asked me if I would drive him down to US Highway 6 so he could hitch-hike back toward Washington. He asked me not to let anyone know of his plans. He had tried to get the used car dealer to take back his big car, but they wouldn't take it until he paid considerable more on it; if he didn't, they would have the sheriff on him.

The next morning I waited on him for a long time and he finally showed up coming in from the west. He had circled the town so the dealer wouldn't see him carrying his suitcase. He wasn't wearing a false mustache but the way he slipped in and urged me to get going, I think he expected a posse to come for him at any time. I drove him the ten or fifteen miles down to US Highway 6 and pointed him in the right direction. I hope he made it, but I never heard from him again.

When the minimum of one year at Montezuma was up, I was given the promotion to Chief of the communication station at Cassoday, Kansas. It was a boost of another forty dollars per month in salary but it was putting us a greater distance from our previous homes. On January 15, 1942 I took over at Cassoday. Arabella and I made the trip without Olive. I had no home for her since I had never been in Cassoday or even in Kansas and we were expecting our first child early in March. She returned to her parents' home to await that event.

Courtesy of Cassoday Cafe

Cassoday, Kansas

Cassoday and Kansas was a new experience. The town had a population of about seventy-five and it was a cow-town set in the beautiful flint hill or blue stem grass country. The town's streets were of dusty gravel; what sidewalks existed were board walks and the business district – what there was of it – consisted of wooden, mostly unpainted one story buildings with Western false fronts. When I first arrived, there was Turk Harsh, in a ten gallon hat, leather vest, rolling his own cigarettes while astride his white stallion. I knew I was in cow-country. It later turned out that Turk was about the only person there who wasn't a cowboy.

We were concerned about the Kansas climate. I was told by one operator who had been stationed there that the wind blew incessantly and that you could be knee deep in mud and have dust blowing in your eyes. That was an exaggeration as there wasn't enough soil over the flint bed rock to ever be even ankle deep in mud. There were practically no cultivated fields anywhere around Cassoday so about the only dust was that raised on Main Street when an occasional car or Turk's prancing stallion went by.

Actually we enjoyed the climate. On a hot summer day the temperature might get up above ninety degrees but because of the green pastures, it wasn't unbearable and we were never without a breeze. This was before we had air-conditioning but we didn't need it when the sun went down; the breeze continued and before morning you would need a blanket. Yes, we enjoyed this Kansas changeable weather.

One beautiful sunny January day about a year after I arrived, Olive, I and our new family addition, Carolyn, drove to El Dorado. The temperature was around sixty-five to seventy degrees and we marveled at how pleasant it was and how we didn't experience that kind of January in Illinois or Iowa. This was on a Thursday, I believe, but on Friday a cold air mass moved in and by Saturday we had a real snow storm with a blizzard following on Sunday and temperatures got down briefly to seventeen degrees below zero. Monday it moderated and by Tuesday the snow had melted. On Wednesday we again drove to El Dorado on a sunny balmy day with sixty degree weather, marveling at what a lovely January Kansas had.

As I previously said, I came to Cassoday in January but Carolyn didn't arrive until March 23 by cesarean section with Olive having a rough time indeed. I went

Cassoday, Kansas

back to Iowa briefly but the ordeal was over before I got there. I returned to Kansas and some six weeks later Olive's parents brought her and Carolyn down. I had rented a house by that time. It was the absolutely only abode available and had been untenanted for a long time except for a sizable colony of mice. Of course the house was not modern: without running water. Our well was back of the house. I had bought six mouse traps and baited them with peanut butter. After we retired we could hear the traps snap. After six snaps, I would get up, empty the traps and reset them. I think my record was some ten or eleven in one night.

After several months a much newer house became available but it wasn't modern either. It looked like a better house and didn't have mice.

It was while we lived in Cassoday that my draft number came up. We were in Montezuma when war broke out, but I was married before that time and while I had no great aversion to enlisting in the Air Corps, I didn't have any great desire to do so. However, the CAA made up my mind for me. Because of the rapidly expanding need for air craft communication and weather reporting, the CAA issued a decree that went out to all stations. This decree stated that anyone resigning from the CAA to go into the armed services would not only be terminated but they would have no re-employment rights thereafter.

I guess this was legal when issued, but when the war ended, Congress passed legislation that required reemployment of servicemen who wished for their job back. Of course I believed them at the time, and so when my draft number came up, I advised our headquarters at Kansas City. They told me not to report and that they would see to it that I was reclassified as deferred because of essential employment. I suppose I had some slight feelings of guilt but had I been drafted I probably would have continued doing the same work but under a different government agency. They had rivalry between government agencies then in war time just as they do now.

I did get an invitation from the Air Corps for a commission to pilot gliders. They probably sent these invitations out to everyone who had a private pilot's license. At any rate this didn't interest me even if the CAA hadn't issued their decree. I never cared for one-way tickets especially if the destination was behind enemy lines. If the order came to retreat, I would wish for enough horse power to get back home.

I don't recall how long exactly we were at Cassoday. It was of course war time and we had rationing of gasoline, sugar, meat, tires, automobiles. Arabella stood the test of time until certain parts could no longer be obtained. We then got a Chevy Coupe from Olive's sister, Elizabeth. We couldn't go far from home but we enjoyed our stay at Cassoday. There was no golf course but the high school had a tennis court and I played quite a bit of tennis with Paul Hilger, my assistant chief. We also hunted ducks and though meat was rationed, Olive got tired of roasting wild duck. I believe we were at Cassoday about a year and a half when I applied for a transfer in grade to Chanute, Kansas. It was for assistant chief at larger station and larger city. We were at Chanute for the reminder of my tenure with the CAA.

Chanute, Kansas

At Chanute we bought our first house. It was an old house, but I got it for $2,300 and borrowed the same amount from the bank to remodel it. I put on a new roof, asbestos siding, rebuilt the front porch, laid hardwood floors, remodeled the bathroom and weather-stripped the windows. When we left, I sold the house for six thousand dollars.

It was at Chanute that our second daughter Nancy was born by caesarian section on April 2, 1945. It was also at Chanute where an elderly lady called to say she thought I was a relative since her maiden name was McCannon. It turned out she was right. Hattie Wheatley was a half-sister of my grandfather. She had left Illinois sixty-five years earlier as a young bride and came to Chanute before it was a town. She came in a covered wagon and never left.

Like Cassoday, we enjoyed every minute of our time at Chanute. We had so many friends there. During the war years I had to work six days a week; with military traffic, airline and civilian traffic we were busy indeed. Suddenly when the war was over, our work fell by half and our personnel doubled. It was then that the petty political conflicts surfaced and bureaucracy began to dominate. Olive and I could see no great future in the CAA so we considered our options.

It was Olive who suggested veterinary medicine with my rural background. We drove to Manhattan and conferred with the Dean of the veterinary school – E.E. Leasure. The Dean encouraged me but gave no promises. He just said that if I could present good grades for the two years of pre-med, I would be seriously considered.

We went back to Chanute and I enrolled some two weeks late in the junior college there. Although I had four years of college, very little could be counted in the medical field – only the electives. The junior college allowed me to take five hours of inorganic chemistry, five hours of physics, five hours of zoology and two hours of speech. I also took a one hour course in poultry by correspondence from Kansas State.

I kept my job with the CAA by going on the midnight shift and working until 8 a.m. The problem was my first class zoology, my easiest course, began at 8 a.m. The teacher was aware of my work conflict and while I received the highest grade on every exam during the semester and got an A+ in Lab, she gave me a B for my semester grade. I protested to no avail since she was rather against my entering her class two weeks late; however, I got A's in all the rest although I'm not sure I deserved it in physics. The grades weren't too bad.

That was all I could get at Chanute so I had to resign in January and enroll at Kansas State for a semester. There I took another five hours of inorganic chemistry, five hours of organic chemistry, three hours of genetics, three hours of parasitological and one hour in the poultry lab. As I recall, I got B's in the three hour courses but A's in the rest. At any rate along with my transfers from

ISNU I had enough to complete the two years pre-med and immediately apply for the professional school the next fall.

When I left for Manhattan, our family was again apart. Olive took the girls back to Iowa and began teaching again. By this time they allowed married female teachers. I was in Iowa that summer and worked as a carpenter for Bill Reiter. It was a tense and anxious summer waiting for word from the college. It was in August, when I had about given up, I got word from Dean Leasure that I was among sixty-five chosen out of the two hundred students who qualified and applied to be selected for the fall semester. Had I known the odds, I may have rethought leaving the CAA.

But, I was in veterinary school.

Veterinary School

In September 1949, I entered Kansas State for the four years of the professional school in Veterinary Medicine. Like Cassoday, there was little rental housing available even though Manhattan was a town of somewhere around seventeen thousand. A student population of about five thousand accounted for some of the shortage, and of course, the recent war caused shortages of everything.

I don't know how I found out, but I heard that the Methodist parsonage at Garrison, twenty miles north of Manhattan in the Blue River Valley was to be auctioned off on a particular Saturday. Even though Kansas State was playing Colorado at home in football that day, I drove up to attend the auction. I never bought anything in my life by auction, but I needed a house. We had settled for the sale of our Chanute house so we did have a little cash available, but I had no idea what the house was worth or how much it would bring.

The owner of the Peterson farm, adjoining the house opened the bidding for $1,800. I bid $1,805 and the sale was over. I had bought the house. I even got back to Manhattan in time to see the second half of the football game.

Veterinary School

Of course the house wasn't modern, but it did have a well with a pump in the kitchen. There was a run-down barn and chicken house, and some acreage of very fertile soil. In fact the property made up a city block. We reverted somewhat to the subsistence farming similar to my grandfather's day on Maple Avenue. We bought a number of pullets and young chicks so we had eggs and poultry in the form of fryers. After I caponized a large number, we had the large lazy but choice roast capon. Chester Thompson had a pure-bred herd of Jerseys, and he brought two Jersey cows for us to keep. We fed and cared for them and got all the milk and the bull calves. His share was of course the cows and any heifer calves they had. We bought a second hand electric cream separator for twenty-five dollars so had all the milk and cream we wanted. We sold cream, along with some eggs, for some cash. We had a large and productive garden; a friend came in with his tractor and lister and plowed and planted the rest of our land to corn. I've never seen any better corn even in Iowa or Illinois.

With money made from extra corn and skim milk, though we also gave some away, I bought young pigs. I think we raised a total of five: some we sold and some we butchered.

When Olive and the girls came down, she got a job teaching school at Stockdale, halfway between Garrison and Manhattan. I would leave her at school as I drove to Manhattan and pick her up returning home. Mrs. Thompson looked after the girls when they were not in school and until we returned.

To complete the picture of subsistence living while in veterinary college, I'll mention that I enlarged the tiny basement, digging and carrying out the soil by hand until we had room for a coal furnace I bought used for five dollars. A most generous friend, Orel Glunt who had a ranch not far away up Dry Creek and I made wood for fuel to burn in winter. He furnished the trees (Hackberry and Oak), circular saw to cut down the trees and a buzz saw on his tractor to cut up the wood, and I got half the wood to heat most of the winter.

    I would add that it was a beautiful, serene but eerie experience to be making and piling up fuel on crisp November evenings in the woods when at dusk the coyotes in the hills surrounding our timber would set up their concert of howling protests of our invasion of their domain. They were no threat and were rarely seen but their concerts were an experience to be remembered.

    I would describe the Blue River Valley as it was then. The Big Blue arose in Nebraska and wound its way southward to join the Kansas or Kaw River (the Indian word) at Manhattan. The valley was mostly about a mile and a half wide with rather steep but not too high escarpments on either side of the river. The rich bottom land was as fertile as any soil in the United States. Up the steep hillsides and stretching away into both directions were the Kansas blue stem grasslands, with timber on the slopes and along the many creeks leading into the valley. It was ideal for mixed farming and ranching as fabulous yields of corn and alfalfa could sustain the herds when the summer grazing was over.

    The people were predominately Swedish, most friendly, as all Kansas seemed to be, and most were descendants of the settlers who bought the land from the Indians or had deeds signed by A. Lincoln from the government. Generosity was a way of life with most. We gave vegetables, especially sweet corn to Bob MacAninch but he would take no pay for plowing and planting our acreage. Oral Glunt would accept no remuneration for our fuel or for feeding our one calf we butchered; but I did repay him one time.

I was a junior in school when Oral called on me one bitter morning in January. He had a Hereford heifer calve during the night and she was down, had expelled her womb and it had frozen to the ground. I told him I would go down to the college and get materials to try to help her. I started, but decided she might not last until I got back so turned around and with no equipment other than a strong curved needle, a pair of scissors and a lot of warm water we thawed the frozen tissue in contact with the ground. I was very lucky; I got the uterus back inside and turned correctly. With the suture material of white sheeting I got her sewn up though I had no anesthesia. She did get up and I am sure she survived.

I did a little practice, but very little and with no pay, around Garrison while I was in school. I delivered my first calf when a rancher insisted that he could get no veterinarian for the job. I treated Carnahans' steers for shipping fever — with permission from Dr. Oberst, one of my instructors. Sulfa was not being used and gave wonderful results at the time. I also spayed a dog for an acquaintance, but that was for small animal surgery credit.

Our part of the Blue River Valley is no more. The Army Engineers had long desired to build a dam across the valley north of Manhattan and when the big flood came in June, I believe in 1952, and flooded cities along the Kaw, the job was authorized. Damming the tributaries of the Kaw was supposed to save the cities below from flooding.

At any rate, Olive was chosen to teach in Manhattan, a good school system. We left Garrison and got married-student housing in the barracks, left over from military days, for our senior year. We sold our Garrison property to the Army Engineers as they were buying up land to go under the lake to be formed.

I figured since it was the government, I would inflate my asking price. I had been trying to sell out trying to double my investment at $3,600 but was unsuccessful as buyers knew the dam was going in. So when the Colonel asked what I would accept, I set my price for the house and all the city lot adjoining at a total of $4,800. A couple of weeks later, I received my answer. The government offered me $5,000. I accepted!

The memory of Garrison was not that of our seemingly primitive existence nor of our good fortune to sell out at a profit as we were about to embark on a new career. No, our Garrison was that of a beautiful valley — the sweet smelling aroma of new-mown alfalfa, the haunting chorus of unseen coyotes and of numerous and unforgettable generous friends.

Going through college for the second time, with fifteen years dividing the two graduation dates, was a bit different but similarities existed, too. The second time had a more specific goal as I was married and had a family and couldn't afford to fail in any respect. Otherwise, veterinary school was such as any school. I had good teachers and mediocre teachers. I had those of outstanding knowledge and ability, and I had those of average knowledge and ability. It was possible to learn from them all.

Dr. Frank was, in my opinion, a poor instructor but he was probably the most outstanding large animal

Veterinary School

surgeon in the country. You could skip all the lectures but read his book and follow him around and ask questions, and you could acquire skill. McLeod was both a good anatomy instructor and outstanding in his knowledge. The same was true of Dr. Mosier. Drs. Hill and Gill were both from the class ahead of me and less experienced but served as good instructors since you could identify with them when you first went out on your own. You learned to handle uncertainties and gain confidence.

My grades were satisfactory thought not particularly outstanding. I got a few C's, several A's in clinics, diagnosis and surgery and a larger number of B's. They were good enough for my name to be on the Dean's list. That meant good enough that class attendance was optional, but when you had to learn all you could that was an option none of the eight on the list exercised.

I guess the only unique accomplishment I achieved was winning both essay contests offered. I won the school prize in both and was second nationally in the contest offered by the National Hospital Association. I was flattered to learn that the doctor in charge of the Boston Memorial Hospital, one of the three judges, had voted mine best. It was my first money earned in my new field. I got a total of $160 and it went towards a fur coat, not a mink, for my wife Olive who helped ease my way through school.

At any rate, in June 1953 on a hot day in the field house some sixty three veterinary students marched up to accept the degrees of B.S. and D.V.M. We scattered to our various ways from California to Indiana, and from Mississippi to Wisconsin.

Olive, the girls and I left immediately for Bloomington, Illinois to open my office there, where the rest of my professional life was to be.

The Large Animal (Farm) Practice

When I was graduated from Kansas State in 1953, most veterinarians were general practice vets. Most of my class were from the farm or from ranches and only a few (including the two girls in the class) intended to specialize in small animal or pet practice. However, everyone took the same courses and our anatomy, physiology, surgery, and clinics covered all species of animals.

Since I had a farm background and communicated well with farmers, I started a new General Practice at Bloomington, Illinois. The three veterinarians in Bloomington-Normal all claimed to be too busy, but all claimed there wasn't business enough for a fourth. If a fourth veterinarian came in, someone would have to leave.

Well things were lean in 1953 but better in 1954 and by 1955 my practice was near ideal. Thereafter I could claim that I had too much practice. I had an advantage. I knew from my younger days many farmers, and my family, were known and especially my brother Dean was well liked; I got many calls because of him. Of course that only helped for the first call. If the client wasn't pleased with your first trip, he wasn't likely to call you again.

Borrowing from my Depression experience, I started out free of debt and with a low overhead and low budget. My wife and my two girls were my entire staff assistants, and that didn't hurt my business. Quite honestly, my practice years continued along the low budget line. My clients did not have to pay for unneeded equipment or for unnecessary personnel.

To put veterinary medicine in proper perspective in 1953 one might liken it to the family physician of twenty five years or so earlier, with certain differences. The doctor of humans needed to know his patient, his patient's family and his art depended on his ability to ask questions, ferret out evidence and signs as well as symptoms and to interpret such data toward a reasonable conclusion. The older physician did not specialize on any particular area of the body or age of his patient. He had fewer diagnostic aids and fewer laboratories to assist him in his art. He depended on his skill, his ability to uncover facts and his ability to interpret all such facts.

The veterinarian when I started out also had to be a sort of zoological detective. He too had to dig out evidence and interpret what he could find. He had a couple of points against him; he couldn't cross examine the patient. Even the myna birds wouldn't tell you where they hurt. And economics entered in. A farmer was unlikely to pay a veterinarian ten dollars to treat an eight dollar ewe.

I think many veterinarians did their best work early in their careers when they had less work so they could spend more time fathoming a situation. When they were less confidant of their infallibility, they worked harder to

The Large Animal (Farm) Practice

uncover more clues and arrived at better and more deliberate diagnosis.

The work of the veterinarian was roughly divided into two general areas, whether large or small animal. There were the preventative and routine duties: consisting of all the vaccination, the dehorning and the trouble shooting side. This latter was the mystery half of the veterinary practice. It, in some cases was quite elementary, but in many cases it was difficult indeed.

The Detective

Deane Riley was one of my many fine farmer clients. He had ponies, swine and a small herd of Angus cattle. He had built a good barn with an automatic water fountain for his cattle and water cups with hinged lids which his pigs could lift when they needed a drink. The water lines were wired to keep from freezing in the coldest weather. This was an improvement from my younger years when we had to chop ice in the tanks or fire a water heater with wood or coal.

He called me on a cold morning early in January. It was about 5 a.m. A few days earlier he had found a dead heifer lying on the railroad ties that formed a platform around the fountain. He didn't call me on that heifer as she was dead, but on this particular morning he found a second heifer bloated and nearly dead in the same spot. Bloat is serious so I hurried down.

When I arrived, he had rolled the heifer over and though she was weak and trembling, she managed to struggle to her feet and was no longer bloated. In the absence of any evidence of infectious disease, I came to the conclusion that the heifers were being electrocuted. Somewhere there was a spot where a metal spike was in contact with a hot wire. How it happened that Deane didn't get some voltage when he rolled the heifer, I don't

The Detective

know but the wiring contractor rewired the job; their insurance paid for the one dead heifer.

About a year later in January, Deane called me to say he believed his pigs had cholera and all were sick and several had died. I didn't feel too good about this since I had vaccinated them for both cholera and erysipelas so again I hurried down. I autopsied two or three of the dead ones and assured him they had neither of the diseases. In fact, they didn't show much of anything. They were all piled up in the warmest corner, very emaciated and hadn't eaten for a week. As I stirred them up, a few wobbled over to the water cups, lifted the lid, put their snout in then wobbled back to lie down.

After watching for some time, I saw one of the stronger pigs wander to the open side of the building and when a drop of water fell from an icicle, he licked the ground where it fell. So simple! And yet how easily overlooked! The pigs were dying of thirst. Deane lifted the lids and the water cups were dry. He had forgotten to throw the heating switch when the temperature had gone down to near zero, three weeks earlier and the lines had been frozen since then.

Yes, technology made things easier on the farm but also made things a little more complex. I had another electrical problem at Burdell Slagell's. He had a lone steer in a pen that went off feed and just stood looking at the water fountain. I asked Burdell to test the temperature of the water, and of course he got shocked as I knew he would. We treated the steer by watering it in a bucket and after about ten gallons, it went back on feed.

I had another client who wanted me to come out and see why his steer drank so much water. Sure enough, when I got there the calf was standing at the large water tank and would stick his nose down deep into the water clear up to his eyes. I solved that case quickly when he raised his head and I could see water running out his nose. That animal, too, was dying of thirst. He couldn't swallow.

Cattle will sometimes eat on hedge apples from the osage hedges. One had lodged in this calf's throat. I caught the animal and passed a bovine stomach tube – a rather large stiff hose. It didn't take much jabbing, and I got the apple pushed out of the esophagus into the rumen. Then the steer really did tank up on water.

I had other problems to solve that were not caused by infectious diseases. Poisoning was one – usually lead poisoning. If I suspected lead poisoning, the farmer would invariably deny any possibility of any lead paint available to his livestock. If the animals were on pasture, I would inquire if there were any gullies or ravines where he may have dumped trash, wire or old machinery to act as a dam to control erosion. Usually there was and frequently I would find old paint cans rusted away with the layer of white or red lead looking fresh where the inquisitive calves had licked them clean.

In one particular case, a farmer had lost two or three cows. Actually, he had lost one, had one missing (later found dead a mile from home) and a third one in terminal condition. The picture, as well as the symptoms, of the ill cow suggested lead, but there seemed to be no source. In walking over the lots, I noticed a dusty churned up area and when I walked over the ground I could see traces of ashes. I then asked the farmer if the herd had access to mineral and when he had burned in that area. The cattle did not have mineral available and the ashes were from an old house he had torn down and burned recently; and

The Detective

yes, the boards were painted. The boards burned but not the white lead that made up part of the ashes; the ashes were almost gone. The cattle starved for mineral had ingested almost all the ashes.

The farmer fenced off the burn site, lost no more cattle but could hardly believe lead poisoning until the results of the liver specimen I sent in to the lab came back – confirming a lethal quantity of lead.

I did have one case that tried my skills of deduction. It wasn't a client of mine. He was a sizable cattle feeder southwest of Heyworth. The Heyworth veterinarian called me to ask if I would come down and look over the herd that had him baffled. It was a herd of about a hundred shipped in steers from the West that were on nearly full feed but were not very thrifty; Dr. George said they seemed to have a long standing low grade "shipping fever", many of them running mucus from their noses and a lot of them lame. They didn't show footrot and few of them ran high fevers that did respond to treatment; they just didn't improve.

I examined a few feet, took some temperatures and went in to look around the barns. I found the cattle were being fed two year old silage for their roughage as well as the corn and protein concentrate. A mineral was available free choice but there was no evidence any had been consumed. The owner admitted he hadn't added any mineral as they didn't eat any. He went on to say some of the researchers were touting diphosphate since many cattle feeders with cattle on pasture or on hay weren't using enough phosphorus. He was feeding the diphosphate with the ground corn. This mystery was then solved although I didn't tell the owner or Dr.

George what steps to take until I consulted my *Morrison Feeds and Feeding* book.

The cattle were being gorged on phosphorus and starved for calcium. Silage was high in phosphorus as was corn. Hay and pasture was high in calcium but they weren't getting any. The cattle weren't eating regular mineral but were being forced to eat concentrated phosphorus. After I had worked out the problem, I advised how many pounds of bone meal or powdered limestone they needed to mix in the with ground corn to bring up the ratio of calcium to the proper level. Within two weeks all the lameness and running noses had cleared up.

Caesarian Sections

Every veterinarian has had to do caesarian section many times during the course of his practice years. By far a greater percentage of human physicians have never done a section and those who have – only on one species of animal – Homo sapiens.

In fifteen years of general practice, I have done sections on cattle, sheep, swine, dogs, cats, a chinchilla and one African lioness. This isn't mentioned to boast of skill but rather to indicate that the general practitioner had to do what was required, to improvise when necessary and sometimes to work under conditions that would cause a physician to shudder.

There was Francis Devine. He called me one evening after dark. It was an obstetric call on a Hereford heifer. She wasn't in a barn. It was a wet spring and she was lying in the swampiest area of his pasture. Because of the swamp, we couldn't get near her with a car or tractor and she refused to rise. I put my lariat on her; there was nothing to tie her to. If she did rise, we probably could grab the rope and get her to a barn or at least to a post, but that was no problem. She stayed down.

Well, I found that the calf was dead and the heifer was too small for any normal type of delivery. It had to be a section in spite of the dark night and less than ideal facilities. I gave her a spinal anesthetic, infiltrated the skin area of the flank with Novocain and went about the operation with Francis holding my flashlight to illuminate the field of endeavor. The whole operation took only about forty minutes. We got the calf out, the uterus sewed up and the muscles and skin sutured firmly. I took my lariat off and when I gave her a shot of penicillin, the doggone heifer finally jumped to her feet and ran away. What timing!

I can recall at least three times in cattle when the operation was performed with the patients standing upright. Two of them were dairy cows in stanchion and one even munched a little hay while the operation went on.

I wouldn't want to imply that all such operations were successful but most were. One spring during the pigging season, I did section on five sows. Four survived and one didn't though the indications were poor for two or three. On one of them the owner called me on a Sunday evening after dark – a routine OB call. Harold and Ruth Maurer were at our house so he went with me to look on, but with the first spurt of blood, he remained outside the pig house pacing up and down.

At any rate I found that a neighbor's hired hand had claimed he knew how to deliver pigs and had fixed up a nine pound wire as a hook to catch the pigs' lower jaw and draw them out. His casting wasn't very successful; he didn't hook any pigs but did put the hook through the uterus and tore a big hole. I had to do a section as that hole had to be sutured up. We used a barbiturate for anesthesia, injecting it into a vein of the sow's ear.

Again I had to use my flashlight to perform the operation. I found two dead pigs floating around the

Caesarian Sections

intestines where they had gone through the teat. I delivered two other dead pigs and a couple of live ones, sutured up the tear and the other tissue before retrieving Harold and going back home.

Some two months later I happened to see the owner of that sow in town. He wasn't a regular client and I never made another call at his place; but when he greeted me, I asked if that sow by any chance was still alive.

He said, "Nope". Before I could express regret, he added, "Oh, she got along fine. I just had her butchered last week. She's in the freezer."

As one might surmise from these cases, it frequently happens that an animal that has little chance might surprise us and survive in spite of poor environment and sometimes the animal with the best prognosis failed to make it. I mentioned I had five sections on sows this particular spring, and the most hopeless case, just described, made it. It also happened that the most promising case, a Duroc gilt in good shape with an easy clean surgery, got up from her anesthesia, went out, drank, ate and went inside – lay down and died.

Caesarian sections in dogs were usually successful. They were usually done in my office with better asepsis. Ether was used as it was safer on the puppies. Usually one of my daughters gave the ether, rubbed and revived the offspring as they were delivered. The girls rather liked to do it, especially if a friend was there so they could show off. On one occasion Buzzy Smithson was watching for a while until he felt a bit faint. He had to leave and sit down, much to Carolyn's amusement and glee.

One client raised purebred Manchesters and miniature dachshunds. I used chromic catgut for sutures as it held well but would eventually be absorbed, and the dogs would not have to be brought back for the sutures to be removed. At any rate this client brought in his dachshund that I had done a section on six months earlier. No problem with either operation except that the previous sutures were still in place and I removed the old sutures before adding a new set.

The lion operation I inherited from an older veterinarian who wouldn't make a try. The problem was to get her anesthetized. I had to rig up a pole with a syringe on it and try to get it in when she got within range. It was a crude method and I know she got considerably more than she needed as she slept for about two days afterwards. Dick Streckfuss, the newspaper reporter wrote, "Working before zookeepers, two nervous male lions and his nervous wife, Dr. McCannon delivered a dead cub in an operation lasting half an hour."

Delilah, the lioness, after coming to went to the outdoor cage to sun herself and I went in and gave her a bottle of glucose and another shot of penicillin. The following day she was again pacing the cage and I wouldn't have gone in with her if they offered me the whole zoo. John Bray asked if I would be coming back later to give her anything more. I said to him, "No, but if you want to, you can bring her to my office and I'll treat her some more."

At any rate I will not go into too many more of my individual or interesting cases but turn more to the people with whom I dealt. After all, the human animal is as fascinating as the lower species.

Thornton Thorpe's Stallion

When I started in practice, I did not expect to do much horse work. I assumed that the day of the horse was passed except for an occasional pet. Actually the horse practice grew. With the pony fad, pleasure horses, show and race horses, the horse practice passed sheep and poultry though it never surpassed swine and cattle in volume. I didn't invest in casting harness. I thought if I did happen to get a call to castrate a stallion, I might borrow the harness from one of my competitors.

Well, in the early lean months of 1953, I received a call from Thornton Thorpe of Wapella. Thornton was a cousin of my mother's and lived about a mile from our home on The Avenue. He always had good horses and his white stallion Silver King pranced at the head of a parade when the Chicago World Fair opened in 1933. This horse was also the sire of my favorite, Silver Legs.

"Charles", he said. "This is Thornton Thorpe and I hear you have become a veterinarian." After I admitted this was true, he went on, "A bunch of us down here still like horses and we have a few stallions that should be gelded. I've got a five year old chestnut stallion that's getting too mean to handle until he's gelded. The trouble is we can't find a veterinarian who will castrate them standing. They all insist on using the Casting Harness. That bangs them up when they're thrown and sometimes leaves them with bad rope burns on their fetlock joints. Tell me Charles, do you ever geld these horses standing?"

Now I believe in honesty and truth; yes, I also needed the business so I answered him truthfully. "Thornton, I've never castrated one any other way." Fortunately, he never cross-examined me on the extent of my experience.

The next day when I entered the barn, with my scalpel, emasculator and disinfectant, and viewed that big brute – hopping up and down, snorting and trembling – I rather wished for some excuse to call off the operation. I didn't hop up and down or snort, but the horse and I trembled together.

Now Dr. Frank, our well-known large animal surgeon at Kansas State, always used the casting harness for the job, but Dr. Gill, a year ahead of me in school, had read of the standing operation and wanted to try it. In clinics I was in Gill's group when he tried it so I had seen it done. However, this was my first experience at gelding a horse by any technique. I hoped I remembered how Gill did it.

We blindfolded the horse, tied up his tail and with Thornton holding a twitch on the stallion's nose; I had the operation over in five minutes. The horse never offered to kick. The next time I saw Thornton he said he never had a horse get over the operation so quickly.

I never did get around to buying a casting harness! From that time on, I dominated the gelding profession. I gelded as many as forty horses in one season. At least twice I did the job with no help around. I never lost a patient or got kicked during the procedure. Both Dr.

Little and Dr. Bane had me demonstrate the technique, but neither of them ever tried it themselves.

Smokey

Smokey was a farmer well pleased with his lot. He was proud of his late model Buick, the pickup truck that he had bought at a bargain and cobbled into workable order, his herd of Hereford cattle, and his wife. One did not have to cultivate his society for any extended period to discover this inordinate satisfaction with his share of life's bounty. Usually ten minutes in his company, and any stranger could suspect it. To preclude any possibility of misunderstanding, Smokey's opinions were delivered with an air of no rebuttal accepted and clinched with a stiff finger poking the chest of the listener in cadence with his words.

Smokey's neighbors accepted Smokey and his blustering opinions with tolerant amusement. Away from his company they could dismiss with a smile all his claims to superior possessions, but no one disputed his claims as regards to his wife. She was slim, handsome, and rich! In extolling the excellence of his position, Smokey usually listed his wife third just behind his Buick and his livestock, but with others she rated as an "only" asset. And this was completely without envy. For you see Smokey was really two persons. Not a "Dr. Jekyll and Mr. Hyde", but simply an indoor and an outdoor "Smokey". Outdoors he could proclaim the excellence of

Smokey

all that was his and how simple it would be to solve such world problems as Afghanistan and the National Debt; but indoors material ownership was in completely different hands and opinions were withheld until cleared by the censor.

My first contact with Smokey occurred on a pleasant spring day when he called for me to come out as he had a heifer that needed "cleaning". Now for a farmer, the term "cleaning" needs no explanation, but for the uninitiated it means removing the retained placenta or "afterbirth" after a cow had calved. I think with all veterinarians they can list duties they dislike more, but "cleaning" certainly is down near the bottom of the list of routine chores. The problem is that a period of time—usually from two to three days should elapse after calving before the job should be accomplished. If it could be successfully done right after calving, the animal would eliminate the membranes without professional help, and if they weren't cleanly removed, the remnants became a source of later infection. So you waited three days for the attachments to "ripen", and in warm weather they became very "ripe" indeed! Even with the use of rubber gloves and a shoulder length sleeve there tended to linger an essence that would never be mistaken for "Attar-of-Roses"!

Having ascertained that sufficient time had elapsed, I inquired as to the location of the stable where I would find the heifer. Smokey then informed me that she was in a forty acre pasture east of the house. I endeavored to impart the information that I had no cowpony, my lariat was only thirty feet long, and that I was not particularly swift afoot, and thus would need work in an enclosure considerably less than forty acres. It was at this point that I was informed on the sterling qualities of this outstanding herd. He described how gentle and affectionate all his cattle were. He could drive his pickup among them and they would come up crowding around to be petted and have their ears scratched. It was my opinion from his dialog that I should have more concern about over-friendliness than aloofness. Feeling somewhat guilty for entertaining such childish doubts, I told him I would be right out.

Upon arrival Smokey, after viewing my Chevy with obvious disapproval and suggesting that I had never driven a car until I drove a Buick, said that I had best put my equipment in his truck, as the cattle were familiar with it. We entered the pasture and slowly approached the herd. Their heads all came up and when we got within fifty yards, they scattered like a flushed covey of quail. It occurred to me that obviously none had itchy ears that morning that wanted scratching. Smokey stopped the pickup and called to them in endearing terms, but you would have thought that the cattle had mistaken him for Gus the butcher, the way they kept their distance.

Smokey then conceded that his cattle were cleverer than he thought, and that they recognized that he had a veterinarian in the cab. However, since the heifer was basically gentle, if I would just climb in to the back of the truck with my lariat, he would just drive up along side her and I could drop the rope over her horns—no problem. I had just known Smokey a little over ten minutes, but already I had that sinking feeling that—well, it's going to be one of those days. But I climbed in and the great chase began. I don't believe the heifer could be gently approached, and even if she could

Smokey

have been, the impulsive Smokey was not the one to do it. The heifer started at a brisk trot, but with the roar of a noisy motor as the foot feed went to the floor, she broke into a headlong gallop for the more distant reaches of the pasture. Paraphrasing Mr. Kipling's poem:

"The truck it fled, like a stag of ten,
The heifer like a frightened doe."

Not that I was contemplating at that particular moment either poetry or the joys of the chase, for the meadow was not exactly as smooth as the beach of Daytona, and I was grimly hanging on trying to avoid being tossed from the bouncing truck. Smokey had pride in his cattle, but he also thought highly of his pickup, and no thousand pound Hereford was going to escape him. As the two unlikely antagonists flew across the pasture, I gave no thought to my lariat as I was using both hands trying to cling to my mount. I couldn't have stood to throw the rope, and had I done so and successfully caught her with the rope secured to the truck it could have resulted only in a tangle of metal, beef, and veterinarian! A result that held little allure. So I just held on, admired the form of the fleeing heifer and wondered if the pickup had brakes when we arrived at the far corner.

However, I didn't even have to fake a throw. The heifer was stretched out in a fine gallop with ears flattened and tail and four feet of afterbirth streaming out behind. The truck was winning and as we pulled even to the heels of the heifer, she elected to evasive tactics and made an abrupt right angle turn. We were all traveling at high speed north by northwest, but after the turn the heifer traveled east by northeast and the truck, the veterinarian, and the afterbirth continued north by northwest!

I rapped on the cab and got Smokey stopped. He demanded to know why I hadn't caught the heifer. After all, he had pulled up close to her!

"Well Smokey," I said. "She was such a gentle creature, and I didn't wish to disturb her placid disposition so when you drew up to her, I just reached over and cleaned her as she galloped along!"

No more than a week elapsed when I got my second call from Smokey. One of his cows had foot rot and it was getting bad. Upon inquiry I found that yes indeed she was in the forty acre pasture. "But Doc," he said, "you won't have any trouble catching this old gentle cow."

"Well Smokey," I replied, "if there is one thing I dearly love to do—it's a good chase to lasso cattle. However, I just don't have the time. You will have to get her in."

"But Doc," he explained, "I can't get her up to the barn. She can't even walk. She's down, and I can't even get her up. You won't have any trouble with her."

It was with some misgivings that I told him I would be right out. This time I had my lariat in my hand when I went over the gate and as before the herd scattered like thistledown. The last and biggest cow eyed me, then struggled to her feet. She did indeed have foot rot, and her left rear foot was about the size of a melon. She did, however, still have three sound legs—which was fifty percent more than I had—and a fourth very painful foot

Smokey

in reserve if needed. She could keep just tantalizingly out of my reach and did so without displaying any good racing form. We worked the herd into one of the pasture corners and since the lame cow was closest to us, when she turned to size up the situation, I threw the rope which settled over her horns. In spite of the fact that Smokey yelled, "We got her!" and stampeded the rest of the herd, I managed to swing around and get a precarious half-hitch around a stout post. We just barely had her. I was at one end of the rope and she at the other some twenty-five feet way. We were at what could be called an impasse, and I couldn't get Smokey to understand how to get behind her and quietly work her closer to the post. His yelling and waving his hat only made things more difficult and didn't do much for either my precarious hold or the cow's disposition.

Finally he said, "Doc, let me hold that rope and you work her up. She sure can't get away from me."

I explained that when she moved, the rope would slacken and the half hitch would permit him to pull the rope tight until she could be worked in where we would have her secure and tight enough to work on. I said, "Now Smokey, don't let her get any slack. There's a weak spot near your end of the rope so if she gets any play and momentum, she'll be gone."

"Don't worry Doc," was the rejoinder. "She sure won't get away from me."

Now experience is a great teacher. This profound statement is not denied by many, but the aptitude of learners by experience does vary, and there are times when I consider my own aptitude for such learning to be suspect. This was one of those times. I had at this point known Smokey for over an hour and was still gullible to think he could follow any instructions other than his own.

I got behind the cow and placed my hand on her hip; she started moving forward and to the left. She felt the rope slacken, so she broke into a trot, then swung to the right, picked up speed, and with me yelling, "Tighten her up!" and Smokey yelling, "I got 'er, I got 'er." Her twelve hundred pounds came to the end of the rope. It snapped and she galloped away with my rope dragging behind. Smokey, instead of keeping the rope tight, had knotted it so that it couldn't pull out of his hands. He looked at the remnant and pronounced, "Very inferior material."

At this point I might digress a bit on the matter of roping and lariats. Now it is true that in my childhood days in the era of Tom Mix, Jack Hoxie, Hoot Gibson and other heroes of the Western Movies, my sole ambition was to grow up to be a cowboy complete with faithful horse, six-shooter and lasso. This ambition had departed by the time I was in sixth grade, and I realized I was in error—that professional baseball was a more glamorous vocation. Not too long after I went into general practice on the prairies of Illinois, the realization suddenly came that at last I was a cowboy. I still never owned a six-shooter and I rarely ever got on a horse, but my lariat was my constant companion and a tool of my profession as surely as was the syringe and scalpel. Modestly, I could claim to be an expert with the rope. Skill is a relative thing. In Wyoming I would never have the confidence to test my roping skill, but here it had to be used, and no one else could throw a rope, so I had to be the roper.

Smokey

My choice in lariats in those early years of practice was what was called a "Blacksnake" treated hemp. It was tough and of small diameter and best for accurate throwing. Its drawback was the lack of durability. It would take about three weeks of use to get it into best working order and seldom would last me more than six months. This was not because it wore out that soon, but because of the necessity of hitching it to available stout beams or posts with hard sharp edges that cut fibers and started a fraying of the rope. In later years I switched to nylon ropes both for safety and economy. Though they cost more, they never cut or wore out. They weren't as good for throwing, but at this stage, I wasn't so anxious to display my roping skill.

But back to Smokey and the blacksnake rope. The rope did have a weak spot but it also had plenty of service left had directions been followed. At this point I was a bit more irked than somewhat, so I told Smokey to open the gate, that I had an older backup rope and we would handle the cow in the barn. He said well since I had another rope and had no trouble catching her the first time, we would certainly hold her the next time. I got the rope; we crowded the cows in a second corner and I caught her again on the first throw. This time there was no post handy, but we got her snubbed to the bumper of the pickup. We worked her up fairly close and I got a needle in her hip, but before I could get any antibiotic in, she sawed the rope in two on the sharp bumper and galloped away with two of my ropes and one needle. At this point I turned to Smokey and said, "Smokey, at this point I should go home, and you can call me again if by any chance you can see your way clear to get the cow into your barn. However, I've got too much equipment attached to that cow. Open the gate; we're driving her in."

Thirty minutes later I was on my way home. My equipment—such as it was—had been retrieved; the cow was treated and my spirits and humor had been revived. I found that Smokey had livestock about which he hadn't previously boasted. The little-used barn had been invaded by a colony of the biggest, the most ferocious and the most handsome bumblebees in the community. Smokey in his noisy way somehow irritated them, and two had nailed him before he could get through the door.

The Towanderosa

The first time Charlie Brokaw called me for assistance, he identified himself as, "Doc this is Charlie Brokaw from Towanda, and I find myself in immediate need of your professional services. Can you see your way clear to coming up here right away?" Having established his identity on this occasion, his usual breezy calls over the many years subsequent to this first call varied according to his mood or to current events. It frequently was..."This is Charlie Brokaw of the Towanderosa. I wonder if that six weeks' correspondence course you took in veterinary medicine may have touched on the problem that seems to have inflicted my fine herd of cows."

You see this was about the time that the television series *Bonanza* became popular with the Cartwrights and their ranch "The Ponderosa". He even had a very large and strong individual working for him, whom he promptly rechristened "Hoss".

All my calls to the Towanderosa were very educational, were enjoyable, and anything, but dull. The Brokaws had a registered herd of Herefords, comfortable barns, beautiful oak pastures, and an unlimited supply of observations and stories. Charlie was willing to dispense all news and explanations of his neighbors, local and national government, politics, and the economy. Each call would likewise yield at least two or more off-color stories—most of which I hadn't heard previously.

That first call mentioned above was on an obstetric problem and awakened me a few minutes before midnight on a pleasant spring night. I found the farm without any problem, and the heifer needing delivery was in a warm well-bedded stall with most of the Brokaw family in attendance. Charlie expounded on the pedigree of the heifer and announced that since she had been inseminated by the best and most expensive Hereford bull in the United States, it was imperative that we deliver a live offspring. He volunteered a bonus of a fifth of whiskey for a live delivery and would double that if it were a bull.

Now the bonus offer (which incidentally was never received) had no particular attraction except to cause me to be a bit more nervous. In the examination, I found the calf was alive and no exceptional problem presented itself, except the head and forequarters of the calf seemed too large. Nevertheless, I maneuvered the fetus into the correct position, and with considerable traction we had a successful delivery. The calf was big-boned, healthy and it was a bull. Everyone, even the heifer, seemed well-pleased.

The problem became evident later. The calf failed to grow. It turned out to be a genetic dwarf!

The second call I got from the Brokaws was about two weeks later. It was not at midnight. As a matter of fact, it was only a few minutes past eleven. Again it was

The Towanderosa

an OB case that Charlie invited me on. He mentioned in his broad-minded way that he didn't hold me entirely responsible for delivery of the dwarf and was willing to give me another chance.

Owing to the bad habit of retiring about ten thirty most nights when I could, I had to arise and dress and make the fifteen mile trip. It was about 11:45 when I arrived, and the Brokaws met me at the car. Charlie said he and the heifer decided I was taking too much time, so he had tied a rope on the calf's legs and to his pickup truck thus the calf had already arrived and was in good shape. After offering my congratulations, I remarked that since I had nothing else to do, I would just go back to bed.

At that Charlie said, "Well, no Doc, don't leave yet. It just happened that when I pulled that calf, I pulled the womb out too. I'd appreciate it if you would put her back together before you leave."

The third call from the Brokaws must have been a few weeks later because it was warm and summer had arrived. It was earlier in the evening—only about 10:00 p.m. because I hadn't yet gone to bed. Yes indeed this was Charlie Brokaw calling from the Towanderosa, in urgent need of an obstetrician. I advised him that I would not have to dress since I had not yet gone to bed, so he could expect me at least five minutes sooner than my usual time. He advised me to take my time, that both he and the cow were the acme of patience and would await my arrival.

When I got there, the family met me at the car and Charlie said, "Well, Doctor, I have good news and bad news. The good news is that it is a warm night, no rain; we have plenty of warm water and you are among congenial people. The bad news is that we have been trying for two hours to get that stubborn cow in a barn with a complete lack of success. She's out there somewhere in that five acre lot, so you can demonstrate whether that correspondence course taught you how to throw a lariat."

It wasn't too difficult to catch the cow. The headlights of his pickup blinded her enough so that I had no trouble getting her roped and secured to the truck. She fought a good fight but tired soon and lay down to continue her futile labor. We had to leave her where she lay, and I stripped to the waist and laid down behind her to go to work. The head of the calf was turned back, so it took appreciable time and quite some work to get the calf turned and coming properly.

I was conscious of some discomfort on my bare chest as I worked and was aware that I was not lying on soft tender bluegrass, but in due time the calf was in proper position and the delivery came easily. After the cow was released and I had washed up, I asked Charlie to put his lights on the spot where I was lying. I wanted to see what my bed consisted of. He said, "Oh, we don't need to do that. You were on what we here at the ranch refer to as 'Irish Clover'. I am told that some people call it Canadian thistle!"

At a later date, in sending a statement to Brokaw, I listed my charges:

Night call: No Charge

The Towanderosa

Obstetric: No Charge
For torture by lying in a thistle patch - $18

    A month must have gone by before I got my next call from Brokaw. The calving season was past. This call was on a sick herd of pigs and came in near nine in the morning of a hot summer day. These hogs were on his second farm a few miles east of the Towanderosa, and I arrived there in mid-morning. Charlie approached the car as I got out, but before he could begin his breezy dialog, I peered at him in a frowning way, finally saying, "I'm looking for a Charlie Brokaw."
    "Come on Doc," he said. "It hasn't been that long since I've called you."
    "Oh," I said, "so you're Brokaw. I wasn't sure. You see this is the first time I've seen you in daylight."

Right Name – Wrong Cow

My sense of hearing leaves a bit to be desired. This doesn't cause me any appreciable inferiority complex. In fact, since quite a bit of our spoken communication if left unsaid would not leave us too impoverished; there are those among us who might lay claim that if they hear half that is said would still hear more than is necessary; nevertheless, the lack of acute hearing can be embarrassing.

It was during the noon hour on a pleasant autumn day and I was in the back yard in some trivial occupation, when my wife called out the back door to inform me that Walter Lay was on the phone and wished to know if I had time that afternoon to come by his farm to dehorn some cattle. I asked her how many he had to dehorn. She said Walter thought he had nine or ten. Well, it happened I had scheduled a blood testing on a small herd out north of Danvers that afternoon and would be pulling my livestock chute for the job and would be returning right by the Lay farm. I told her to tell Walter that I would be there at 3 p.m.

I had no problems or delays on the job at Danvers and at ten minutes to three I pulled into the Lay farmyard. Walter and Marvin Lay were working on a corn combine and left the machine to greet me.

Right Name - Wrong Cow

I could see the horned steers behind the barn but they weren't penned up. I said, "Well, I see you haven't got the steers penned up yet."

Marvin replied, "Well, in just five minutes we will have them behind gates in the back shed, if that's okay."

I said, "That will be fine but it looks a bit muddy in the lot, and I may get stuck. Do you have a tractor to back in the chute?"

They quickly assured me a tractor was available and in a matter of only about ten minutes, the steers were all inside, gated up and my chute was in place; we were in business. The only puzzling problem was that it was very obvious that there were considerably more than ten head of cattle in the dark shed, a fact that I mentioned to them.

The Lays are very agreeable people and again they agreed that yes indeed there were more than ten head of steers. In fact as time went by and the pile of horns grew higher, I looked back into the dark shed and commented that we should be about finished since we had already dehorned eighteen out of those ten head. Marvin gave a polite chuckle though giving the impression that while he didn't quite understand my humor, he was willing to be tolerant. The Lays were good workers and we went very rapidly through the herd of thirty-one steers, removed the horns, stopped the hemorrhage and applied the styptic. The chute was jacked up, and I pulled in home by 5 p.m.

As I was parking the chute, my wife came out and asked me where I had been; what had held me up? I told her there were three times as many as what they said but we finished the job. She then informed me that Walter had called back at 4 p.m. and said it was getting too near chore time so to postpone the trip to the next day.

I then said, "Hey, wait a minute. Walter Lay couldn't have called you at 4 p.m. We were right in the middle of the job."

She then said, "What were you at Walter Lay's for? Your appointment was with Walter Lash."

A week later I was back at the Lays to treat a cow for mastitis. I told them that I had no objection to being considered a bit eccentric but I didn't wish them to consider me fit to be committed so I explained the confusion of identity. "How come you didn't tell me that you hadn't called to have your cattle dehorned?" I asked.

"Oh, we really had intended to have those steers dehorned," Marvin answered, "So when you dove in, Dad said, 'Here's Doc. I'll bet he thinks we had better get those steers dehorned now before the weather gets bad!'"

A second incident of mistaken identity occurred on a cold winter day and was not owing to faulty hearing on my part. My wife was not home that day, and the telephone answering service was taking my calls. I got in shortly after noon and called the answering service to see if there were any calls. They advised me that Mr. Gillis called and that he had a cow with mastitis that he felt I should treat without delay. I told the answering service to hold my calls and I would be back in an hour or so.

Now the Gillis's were among my many really fine clients and it was always a pleasure to respond to their calls. Mr. Ruel Gillis was a dairy farmer out near Carlock, and he had two sons: Bob toward Danvers and Jack at Heyworth. Somehow the term "mister" always applied

Right Name - Wrong Cow

to Ruel and the boys were Bob and Jack so without giving any more thought to the matter, I hurried out to Ruel's place.

When I arrived, there didn't seem to be anyone home but sixteen Guernsey's were lined up in their stalls in the barn. It was never unusual for the farmer to be absent since he usually didn't know the exact time to expect the veterinarian, and this kind of trouble never required assistance in treatment. What was unusual was that there was no note or explanation as to the location of the cow needing attention. Sometime in such situations the farmer might not have paper and pencil handy so he might just chalk a big X on the hip of the cow or if he had no paper or chalk, he always had binder twine handy, he would tie the twine to the cow's tail. Here there was nothing so I had to discover the culprit cow myself.

I started at the south end of the barn and squatting down I examined each quarter for fever, hardness or other abnormality. Believe it or not I went clear down the line and when I finally got to the sixteenth and last cow, I found a very septic right rear quarter. I got the quarter cleaned out, gave the necessary injections and infused the bad quarter with antibiotics. I left Ruel some extra tubes and then wrote out instructions as to when he should next milk out the quarter and infuse fresh tubes. These I left in a prominent place and departed for home.

Upon arriving home I again called the answering service to inquire as to messages. They advised that Mr. Gillis called again and was most anxious that I see his cow that day. This was quite puzzling so I asked if it were Mr. Ruel Gillis that called. All she had was just Mr.

Gillis. I then inquired if there was any mention of where this Mr. Gillis lived. She then said the call came through the Heyworth exchange so I hurried down to Jack's.

I told Jack about my trip to Carlock on his dad's cow and said, "When you next see Ruel, you might explain how he happened to get his cow treated."

The sequel to this story came sometime later on my next trip to Jack's. It seems that when Ruel went to do his chores that night he read the note with my instructions and then hurried to the house and inquire of his wife. "Did you call Doc to come out and treat old Flossie for mastitis?"

"No, I didn't," she replied. "But I told you yesterday that you had better call him. What happened? Did she die?"

"No, she's fine but I'm not! I must have called him because he's been here but I sure don't remember it. I wonder if I'm getting to that state."

The next day he went down to see Jack and confided in Jack that he was beginning to worry about forgetfulness and mental health. Jack didn't kid him much before telling Ruel just what happened. Relief was instant.

Tympany, Hypocalcaemia and Prolapse

Not too frequently, but sometimes it does occur that a veterinarian must choose between two or more emergencies as to which he should respond to first. Naturally, all things being equal one usually went quickly to the one that came to attention first. It was usual that a second or third emergency call came while enroute to or during a first call. Milk fever, pneumonia, obstetric problems, injuries, bloat and a myriad of other problems might come at any hour of the day and might interrupt the veterinarian's sleep, meals or social life. Not infrequently it interrupted my scheduled routine duties, if such work was of rather long duration.

One might think that OB work or disease as pneumonia would be of first priority. Actually, both likely would have been developing for some time, and a delay of some time or even a few hours would usually have little consequence. As an example, I recall receiving a request from a person who was not really a livestock man, but who had a few cows; he wanted my immediate services to deliver a calf. His call came at 9:30 p.m. on a summer night and his communication went something like this: "Doc, this heifer of mine started calving about noon. The feet of the calf showed up about four o'clock so I hooked a rope on them and I've been dragging that heifer around with my tractor since then. I'm not getting anywhere so there's no use messing around anymore. I decided I'd better have you hurry out and finish up."

The main urgency in this case was to stop the torture of the helpless heifer and to terminate the damage already done. I, of course, went out but the problem was not solved until daylight the next day by caesarian section. The point is that the need for prompt response had long passed by. Now I wouldn't want to indicate that this kind of husbandry was usual, but it did occur. I might also add that there was very little hope of recovery for an animal under such an ordeal. Though I have lost cases much more favorable, this heifer did survive.

Milk fever, hypocalcaemia, is one situation that demands instant response. It is one problem that usually minutes, not hours, determine whether it is life or death. It is also one of the most dramatic and satisfactory calls that the farm veterinarian can have if he can arrive in time. This is one of those times that the breaking of speed laws could be morally excused. Every farm practitioner has had that experience of arriving in a rush with intravenous tube, needle and calcium bottle in hand, staring at the downer cow with the glazed eyes then finally seeing a convulsive gasp for air by the cow and knowing then that he had arrived in time. The needle is inserted into the jugular vein and the medicine is allowed to drip carefully into the bloodstream. Frequently, although not always, the dramatics come in perhaps twenty or thirty minutes; the comatose cow with the glazed eyes and rare gasping breath, twitches her

Tympany, Hypocalcaemia and Prolapse

ears, burps a couple of times and then staggers to her feet, and takes a weaving course into the meadow in search of the tender grasses.

Milk fever is brought about by disturbance of the blood calcium. The calcium level in the blood is constant and when milk is formed, the blood yields the ingredients, including the minerals. The blood calcium is instantly replaced, ordinarily from food absorption. However, if there is withdrawal of calcium from the blood and some internal process blocks the calcium absorption, hypocalcaemia or milk fever results. This usually happens in the cow some hours after calving when she comes into lactation. I have, however, treated cows with milk fever a day or two before calving and as long as seven days after calving. While most cases are typical, there are many deviations and not all are easily diagnosed.

Tympany, bloat, is a serious and frequently urgent problem of great economic concern especially in cattle herds on legume pastures in the Corn Belt. Acute or frothy bloat occurs when great volumes of gases are trapped in suds-like bubbles such as in soapy warm water and the gas cannot be eliminated. The rumen or first stomach of the cow is quite large and in a mature animal may hold up to eighty gallons of contents. The ruminant animals do not really digest the cellulose of coarse feeds. Such feed is ingested with large quantities of water and it remains in the rumen for the bacteria and protozoa to break down the fibers into an absorbable nutrient. The rumen convulses or contracts every twenty to thirty seconds to keep the mass stirred up and allowing the gases formed in the digestion to rise and be expelled. The gases are largely carbon dioxide, monoxide and methane.

The rumen is a big fermentation vat. It makes a nice demonstration to light a match at the opening of a stomach tube when those trapped gases are being relieved and the bloated animal shrinks to its normal size.

The bloat becomes dangerous when the gas is trapped. The rumen becomes paralyzed and fails to contract or impaction occurs. The gas keeps on forming and eventually swells the rumen until it presses on the diaphragm and impairs breathing or circulation. Death can occur in a short time when the bloat seems to increase rapidly.

A complete uterine prolapse in a cow is an aftermath of calving, in those cases where the cow continues straining after the calf is born or if some force such as bloat pushes the large dilated uterus backward and it turns wrong side out and is expelled. After this calf bed is pushed out, it increases in size because of fluids gathering due to the impairment of circulation. The organ may increase in size to sixty or more pounds; returning it to its proper position inside the cow is far more difficult than its original expulsion. It's a bit like trying to squeeze and armload of gelatin through a tube half its size. Non-cooperation on the part of the cow, which is usual, makes it a tough job indeed.

I received an urgent call from a client on a dreary spring morning at about 5:30 a.m. Phil lived about twenty miles away, east of Leroy, and had dairy cattle, beef and swine. Like most dairymen, he arose early about 4:30 or 5 a.m. to start his milking chores. When one of his cows that had calved the previous evening failed to show up, he went to find her. He found her stretched out

Tympany, Hypocalcaemia and Prolapse

on a swampy shelf along side a creek. She appeared to be still alive so he rushed in to call me. He said, "Doc, she's in bad shape. She might have milk fever and she's bloated; her calf bed is out in a mass of blood behind her. Do you think there's any hope for her?"

Now one of the minor economies I indulged in was to neglect investing in an alarm clock. The telephone was my alarm. Sometimes it awakened me at 5 a.m.; sometimes it was six and rarely was it later than seven. My medicines and equipment were always packed ready to go so in this instance I was on my way in a few minutes. The road was paved all the way and that early there was almost no traffic so I was there in a short time. Now I mentioned that it was a dreary morning. I meant that it was not only cloudy, but a fine drizzle was coming down and persisted for hours.

The muddy spot where the old brindle decided to go down along side the creek looked churned up as though a couple of playful elephants had used it for mud wrestling. The cow indeed was far gone with milk fever; she was indeed bloated and yes indeed she had a complete uterine prolapse. Thought the arena left considerable to be desired so far as asepsis was concerned, the intravenous treatment for the milk fever quickly removed that problem. By passing the large stomach tube, the bloat was relieved. I had hoped that with these procedures, the cow would have recovered sufficiently to arise and leave her swampy bower. It was not just for me to get out of the fine rain, although I had no objections to that, but it seemed desirable for some degree of cleanup to get the prolapsed uterus out of the mud, blood and manure.

It was not to be. The shock, the exhaustion and the "don't give a damn" attitude of the brindle gave every evidence that she would be content to remain in her oozy bed for a few more days at least. I probably couldn't read her thoughts but it seemed as though the way she looked at me she was saying, "Well Doc, I can rest here till Tuesday if you can."

Phil found a few planks to put behind the cow so that I wouldn't sink clear out of sight and brought many sacks, paper and cloth, along with warm water. I was stripped to the waist, though in the persistent rain, it didn't matter anyway and our battle began. It wasn't a tug-of-war. It was a pushing war. I carefully pushed to start the re-entry and just when I would appear to gain a few inches, she would strain and the slick uterus would pop out on the other side.

Now we have a weapon to help us in such a situation. I had given the cow an injection we call an epidural. It was sort of like a spinal anesthesia to take away pain and stop the straining. It works nine times out of ten and makes the job much simpler; but this was the tenth instance and the cow seemed to strain just from memory.

We had washed up the uterus as best we could when we started and several times afterwards when she managed to overcome the progress we had made. But as time went on and the area became more churned up, any semblance of cleanliness became impossible. We had a good battle – the cow and I – but gradually the straining lessened when Phil's dog yelping at a rabbit under a nearby brush pile seemed to distract the brindle's attention. Suddenly, it was over. The last lump of uterus disappeared inside along with a certain quantity of mud, blood and manure. I didn't remove my arm until the organ was restored to its rightful shape. Sutures were

Tympany, Hypocalcaemia and Prolapse

placed through the tough cowhide and after packing the organ with disinfectants and sulfa powder, the opening was laced with gauze to prevent the prolapse from starting all over.

After washing up and getting into dry clothes, I answered Phil's question. "Not much!"

On Phil's inquiring look, I said, "Two and a half hours ago on the phone you asked me, 'Do you think there's any hope for her?' "

I went on to explain to Phil that the cow would probably get up and come to the barn if she got hungry or lonesome but she won't be worth much if she does survive and there will be massive infection. "She will likely dry up if she does live," I told him. "But if she surprises us and comes along, you can keep her around then send her to market because she can't possibly have another calf."

It was the following winter when I was again at Phil's on some problem and he volunteered the information, "Doc, remember the old brindle cow? I finally sent her to market last week."

I was a bit surprised and answered, "So she made it did she? How come you held on to her this long?"

"Oh, she was giving a lot of milk," he answered. "I hated to send her in but I had to. She was about ready to calve again."

Dog Psychology

The dog is an animal. No one disputes that, no more than to dispute that horses, cattle, birds and all other members of the zoological family are animals. Some people rather abhor being classified as an animal although most would admit that behavior of too much of the human race is lower and more despicable than what we would accept in the animal classes below Homo sapiens.

Actually most of the higher animals have anatomical, physiological and sensory systems similar to the human and in many cases superior. Mankind's domination over all lower animals is based on the power of reason, reflective thought, language and communication. I would not include social behavior as lower animals have a social behavior and even rudimentary communication.

Here I am just considering the domestic dog: the loyal companion and family retainer. As everyone knows, we have affectionate dogs, vicious dogs, useful working dogs, spoiled dogs. The basic difference is completely or I should primarily dependant upon training and discipline. Now there are differences in the psychological makeup and instincts as well as differences in anatomical and sensory abilities among the canines, but I have known

Dog Psychology

able trainers who have made good bird dogs out of mongrels; and the smartest – I should say ablest – stock dog that I ever saw was Spike, a black short hair medium sized dog of indeterminate ancestry.

I saw Spike the first time on a trip to the farm in January to treat some cattle. The Hereford cattle herd was in the corral with the farm gate open to the highway. The gate had been open for weeks since being frozen in that position during a snow and ice storm. I inquired, "What keeps your cattle from getting out on the highway and getting killed or causing an accident?"

"Spike", answered Steve, pointing to the black dog sunning himself by the back door. "No cow would dare go through that gate unless we told Spike to bring them through."

I asked how they trained Spike, and Steve admitted that he didn't do it. A hired man from Kentucky vowed that he would make a stock dog out of the pup that had been dumped at the house. He did so in a brutal way, and Steve admitted they had been on the verge of firing the hired man before the dog learned what was expected of him and remained completely loyal to the family.

On a later trip, I inquired about Spike and his handling of cattle. Steve had bought twenty Western steers and had them on feed; one was to be treated. I didn't have to chase and lasso him; Spike brought in the steer pointed out. Then Steve said, "You want to see something funny? Watch this."

It was feeding time so Steve filled a couple of buckets with corn and told Spike to bring up the steers. The dog rounded up all twenty head and they lined up around the feed trough where the corn was. All the steers began feeding except one that had never tasted corn and wouldn't eat. Nineteen steers fed and one stood among them, his head in the air until all had finished.

Man had trained the dog and Spike had trained the cattle.

Duke

In describing dogs of my personal acquaintances, I should start out with my own. Earlier I mentioned my first dog Herbert which drifted in when I was only four and only stayed a short time until she presented me with a large litter. She ran away with all her litter except my favorite, Brownie, which became my companion for many years through grade school. Brownie and I hunted game, mostly rabbits and explored the countryside until he was run over, near the end of my grade school years.

Most dogs in the rural area were strays that were dumped, by former owners who tired of them, near what might appear as a friendly farm home. My next dog was a purebred tri-colored collie that was brought to us by a town cousin: "Because she was too big for the city and would make a good livestock dog."

Well, I spent hours trying to teach her to round up our milk cows and bring them in without running them or chewing off their tails. I never succeeded. It was soon evident why she was brought to the country, and in due time presented us with eight puppies. Two looked like German shepherds, three were short haired terriers and three looked like collies. Again a chap who dealt in dogs took the whole lot except for my one choice – a German shepherd looking pup which I named Duke.

Duke was a good dog and the best of watchdogs. By being the best of watchdogs I mean he never bit anyone, but if a stranger drove up to our home, Duke would walk slowly toward the gate; the bristles on his neck would arise and without barking, a low throaty rumble would cause the stranger to retreat to his car and announce his presence with a toot of the car horn.

As I say, he never bit anyone, not even me when I performed my first surgery. This was when I was in high school and Duke was following my dad when he was mowing hay. A neighbor's dog sneaked up behind and jumped Duke. In the scuffle Duke got in front of the sickle bar and his right hind leg was severed clear through the bone, only hanging on by some of the skin. His right front leg was badly damaged too.

When I got home from school, my parents told me Duke was probably dead or was dying. I finally found him in a dark corner under the porch and when I saw the damage, I got a razor blade and crawled back under the porch and severed the skin on the back leg. Some two days later Duke came out and hobbled around on two legs – both on the same side. The following winter Duke and I went rabbit hunting together; by this time his front leg had healed to be usable.

I might add that when I took Dad's twelve gauge shotgun, Duke stayed home. If I took a stick that was okay with Duke, but a shotgun - No! That was both a commentary on Duke's intelligence as well as my marksmanship. Anyway we were more likely to bring rabbit home for dinner when the shotgun stayed home.

Duke

Duke was still on the farm when I finished college and left home for Iowa City. He had to hunt on his own and became quite a skunk killer. He kept the skunk population under control. Now if a dog blunders on to a skunk and gets the musk in his eyes, he will never again approach that odiferous animal. If the dog attacks the skunk and kills it, he will always get covered with the scent but will persist in his attacks. Duke came home many times smelling of skunk for the rest of his life.

Eliza

I never had another dog after Duke until I was married and had a family. We then had Smokey, a small black cocker spaniel, until I went back to veterinary school and friends took him. Later in practice I acquired another larger black cocker named Tramp that was a friendly companion for my daughters except she could climb out of any enclosure and would insist on going with them when they went to the lake swimming. They would have to go home as the lifeguard wouldn't let her join in. Even when we kept her tied until they left, she would hunt them out and dive in for her fun in the water.

Now we come to our last dog Eliza. Eliza I got for the girls but she was my dog. I taught her good manners. She would always come when I whistled, would sit motionless (for about ten minutes) on order and dearly loved to play ball. She would shag golf balls for me for hours. She became a good ball player.

She was so friendly she had visitors. Stan Cole, a friend of ours, would sometimes stop by, not necessarily to visit us, but – to play ball with Eliza. Don Hines, a farmer client dropped in one day because his little girl Becky was with him and wanted to stop and play with Eliza. The sponge ball had picked up a needle out of the

Eliza

grass and when Eliza caught the ball, she gave a yelp and clawed at her mouth. I ordered her to stay and she lay there quietly while I opened her mouth and found the needled imbedded in the roof of her mouth. She lay quietly while I went to the office, got forceps, opened her mouth and extracted the needle. She and Becky then resumed their game of ball!

Only one time did I see her in a less than friendly mood. It so happened that there was an accident of a circus truck not too distant and the driver suffered a broken leg. The state patrolmen brought in a half grown lion on a leash for me to care for while the owner was in the hospital. Now the lion seemed friendly and I tied it to a chair in my waiting room. It rested on the chair licking its chops when Eliza arrived on the scene. My wife let her in and Eliza bounded toward the newcomer in her friendly way. Halfway across the room she came to a skidding stop, backed slowly through the door dribbling urine all the way. Once outside with the door closed, she began barking furiously.

The lion cub was with me for two or three days and Eliza stayed clear of the office. After he left, Eliza started coming in again but suspiciously sniffed the chair and cage where the lion was kept and repeated the precaution for some time until the last of the wild odor had left.

Eliza was a sable collie, very friendly and an excellent ball player. She had one bad fault; she was bored about staying home with no one around and if left alone, she would soon leave to seek out where the kids and the action were. One time we were away for a few days and left her in the pen with Danny across the road to care for her. We had hardly gone when she chewed a hole in the fence and took off. When we got home,

Danny was remorseful and had looked all over the neighborhood for her. We had been home a few days and heard from a friend that a new dog and sterling center fielder had shown up in the McClure neighborhood about a mile away. She proved to be the best defensive player on the team.

Well, I called on the McClures and yes, there was Eliza who had now been named Lady; the McClure children had finally convinced their parents that if no one claimed the dog in another day or two, they could claim her for their own and would immediately take her to Dr. McCannon's for her inoculations.

Eliza never left while we were home to give her some attention but left alone, she would soon leave and always found congenial friends so that she never bothered returning home until we went after her. In each case she would greet us with affection, jump into the front seat of the car and ride home happily as though to say, "Nice of you to come and drive me back."

About a block or two away from us was a handsome red-headed boy of about eight that Eliza visited several times to the boy's great enjoyment. He had a fenced back yard and his parents liked Eliza very much also. One time we were going to be gone for a weekend and Olive, who was there to pick up Eliza, asked the boy's mother if they would like to enjoy the dog for the weekend. They would be delighted!

Well, Monday after we returned, Olive said she was going after Eliza. I said, "Now you're not going to take Eliza away from that redheaded boy?"

"Sure," she replied. "She's my dog now that the girls are both in college." Not too long later Olive came back without the dog.

Eliza

"I couldn't do it," she said. "His mother told me the boy wouldn't go to school that day because it was the last day he would have with the dog. I told her if they really wanted the dog, the boy could keep her."

Well, that was our last dog and nearly the last time we saw Eliza as the family moved away not too long afterward. A month or two after giving her away, on a rainy evening there was a noise at the front door and there was Eliza! She never came to our house while we owned her; but from her new home, she had added us to her calling list.

Fritzel

We had special interest in Fritzel. She was one of Tramp's litter, a blonde, "runt-of-the-litter" supposedly cocker although Tramp was black. It turned out Fritzel didn't remain a runt but grew rather tall and had short hair. She did have one of Tramp's characteristics; she was friendly and liked to roam.

Unlike Eliza, Fritzel always returned home from her rambles and spent the night in the house. She belonged to the Warbers – friends of ours – to whom she was given. She was spayed, loved and well-cared for, but she did like to travel.

Now it happened that we had an outbreak of leptospirosis in dogs and although Fritzel had been vaccinated for distemper, hepatitis and rabies, she had not been inoculated against leptospirosis. I had suggested to Eileen Warber that she should bring the dog over for the vaccination. She promised to do so but put it off.

One day I looked out in our yard and there was Fritzel playing with Tramp. I whistled to her and she came into my office so I inoculated her for the lepto. I then wrote out a note saying; "My name is Fritzel and I have been to my doctor and have been vaccinated for leptospirosis".

Fritzel

That evening when Fritzel returned home, Eileen saw the note attached to the collar and thereafter boasted that she had the smartest dog in town. It would go to its doctor when it needed a shot and never had to be forced.

Corky

Unlike Spike, Corky never really had an unpleasant period in his life. That is unless you consider injections for rabies, distemper etc. Corky had the good life: a family that treated him as family. I doubt if he had ever been reprimanded, much less punished. He was a Springer spaniel belonging to the Beichs who owned the candy business.

Now clients had often asked me about training dogs. Of course I never claimed to be a trainer, but I had watched trainers and knew the infinite patience and firmness needed. I always advised dog owners that every dog should understand a few basics - namely the dog should always be trained to come to the owner on command by voice or by whistle. The dog should always "stay" or be quiet and motionless on command. The dog should never show belligerence or bite unless on command. Most dogs thus are basically trained without training. They will come when you call, will quiet down on order and are just naturally friendly. However, some dogs just don't grab the idea that they are a pet or that man holds dominion over them. Some seem to think humans are there merely to provide food, shelter and amusement.

Corky

Corky was one of these. He had a home, unlimited feed and otherwise his was a free spirit. While he was a puppy, the Beichs had brought him in for the necessary injections. Not understanding the desirability of such indignities, he had no love for his doctor. The result of this was that when Patty or Bill would bring Corky to my office for any reason when he got out of the car, no one could get their hands on him. We had many a long visit with the Beichs while either one or the other of them futilely tried to con Corky into letting them touch him. One time they started home then opened a door and he jumped in; thereby got his injection. At other times they would have to go home and eventually Corky would arrive.

One of the last times I heard of him was when someone stole a bike out of the Beich's garage. The garage was where he spent the night. He apparently did not object but when the policeman came to make out the report, Corky bit him.

Baird's Dalmatian

Bob Baird ran a horse boarding stable and arena not far from me, and I had considerable work there as there were twenty or twenty-five horses at all times. He also had a Dalmatian that he brought to my office for inoculations and to be spayed. The dog and I got along well, and she paid me no attention when I called at the stable. The runway between the stalls was her domain, but no one had problems as long as they didn't bother her unless to caress from time to time.

On one occasion Bob called me to treat one of his boarders and while I was there, he mentioned that his dog seemed under the weather and would I check it out. Well, he held the dog and I found she was running a bit of fever with a respiratory problem. I went to my car and got penicillin and gave the dog a shot. This was an indignity in her own runway, in her own barn; when she got to her feet and stalked away, she looked at me over her shoulder with pure and undisguised venom.

Well, I made many trips to the stable afterwards and each time before I could get out of my car she would circle and snarl and I had to watch out, to the amusement of anyone there. She never bit, but she never forgave and never forgot. I could give shots in my office but not to her in hers.

The Biting Peke

A lady who at one time ran the Green Mill Café brought her little Pekinese to me. He was fully mature but was a rather small dog. Her problem was that the dog bit. And she had scars up and down her arms to prove it!

She stated that the Peke was really sneaky about it. He would come to her begging to be picked up and petted; when she did pick him up he would appear loving, but when he wanted down, he would suddenly sink his fangs in her arms. Nothing polite in his manners!

She had previously had the dog vaccinated for rabies; she had come to me to have the dog neutered. She said a good friend of hers had told that castration would cure such ill temper. She would like to know if I thought neutering would help.

"No," I answered. "But it sure would be a good way to get even with him!"

Well, she left the dog for surgery and came back to pick him up the next day. I didn't see either of them for several weeks. Then one day she came back with the dog: this time for euthanasia. She said she sure hated to give up the dog, but it seemed hopeless to break him from his biting. She sure hated to have it done but resolved to unless I had some idea as how to otherwise solve the problem.

I said, "Well, if you really want to keep him, I can pull his teeth." When she understood I meant just the canine teeth or fangs, she went for that.

I didn't see her or the dog for some six months; then one day she came in to get an interstate health paper as she was moving to Montana. I asked her, "Since I don't see scars on your arms, does that mean your dog has quit biting?"

"Oh no," she said. "He still bites, but it doesn't hurt!"

The Saint Bernards

Earlier in this discussion, in describing dog psychology, I mentioned that certain discipline and training was desirable if one were to have a nice companion or useful dog. It did not necessarily have to be brutal discipline such as used on Spike the best cattle dog I ever knew, but sheer indulgence and pampering trained very few "nice" dogs!

The old saying "If you have one dog, you've got a dog; if you have two dogs, no dogs!" is true unless you do have some discipline. Dogs left to their own devices certainly have their own society and if numerous enough they become public nuisances – incorrigible and outside human control.

The easiest thing you can train a dog for, is to make them mean. Tease them to an emotional pitch or merely chain them for life to a stake and you have a mean dog – not necessarily a watch dog – but truly a vicious dog.

The St. Bernard is basically among the friendliest of the canines but I can recall three that were too dangerous to be allowed to live. Two of them became so merely being condemned to life imprisonment at the end of long chains secured to a stake. The third was deliberately made mean. These dogs were sullen and angry with the world. The only humans they would not attack were their owners who brought them food and water. Their mad was against the world. Dogs have instincts but none that I know of have reasoning ability to equate their unhappy existence.

A woman friend of one of these owners went out to admire one of these chained, two hundred pound beauties. She was warned to stay clear but she put her hand out to say "Nice doggy". The "nice doggy" responded by crushing most of the small bones in her hand, pulled her down and got a few ounces of round steak from one of her hips before she could roll free out of range.

On another St. Barnard I had no record of bites, but as animal control administrator for the county, I was called to Heyworth under the complaint of odor nuisance. There was indeed an "odor nuisance". This 220 pound St. Bernard had been locked in a garage for six months with no cleanup during that time. Hot weather had arrived and the aroma could be detected downwind for at least a block or two.

It so happened that the dog owner had answered an ad: "purebred, registered St. Bernard to be given away free to a nice home". He didn't go to see the dog. The previous owner told him he would bring the dog to him. Since they lived fifty miles apart, this sounded like a good deal. The dog arrived in a surly mood so the first owner advised putting the dog in the garage until the dog got used to them.

Well, in six months the dog wasn't "used" to any of the new family. They could throw feed to the dog through the windows since the St. Bernard had broken them out. (They were too small for him to get through.) But when they tried to open the door a crack for a

The Saint Bernards

friendly chat, the dog would hurl himself in frenzy at them. They called the former owner to tell him they couldn't do anything with the dog. He told them, "Well, he's your dog now; I don't want him."

The town marshal had been called, but he was too timid where dogs were concerned so it became my problem. I lassoed the dog when he tried to get to me through the window and with the marshal and the owner hanging onto the rope, I went in and gave the dog an overdose of tranquillizer. The marshal's pickup was backed to the door so I told them to get on the front end and I would lift the dog's back end on the truck. "No way!" said the marshal. "That dog maybe unconscious, but I'm not getting close to his jaws."

Well, I had to take the head end and the two big men got the lighter rear end. I don't know if they ever cleaned out the garage, but I supposed so.

Lest one would get the idea that I was anti St. Bernard, I might mention Mighty Manfred. Bill Frank was an insurance representative and his children wanted a dog. Bill thought it would be cute to get a big one — a St. Bernard — for a conversation piece. He had a fenced in back yard so he bought this cute St. Bernard pup from a kennel in Michigan. I think it cost him one hundred and fifty dollars.

Well, Manfred grew and grew. The bigger he got the less interest his boys took in him and greater became the feed bill. The sanitation problems probably were more irksome than the feed bill. At any rate Bill finally admitted his error in dogs and tried to sell out with a minimum of loss — without success.

Manfred was friendly but when he grew past two hundred pounds, children would run home screaming when Manfred would rear up on his hind legs, lean over the fence and give a friendly "Woof". Bill finally had to give Manfred away for free.

Now the woman that got Manfred had brought many dogs to me for treatment or vaccination. She never was satisfied. She first brought in a cocker then came with a collie saying each time, "This is the kind of dog we really want." After a basenji and spaniel and another collie, she finally took Manfred saying, "We really always wanted a St. Bernard."

She gave away her current dog. A few days earlier she had bought a kitten for five dollars at a pet store then she brought Manfred home.

Well, Mighty Manfred saw the kitten, gave a "woof" and the kitten disappeared into his mouth – only the tail sticking out. The woman gave a scream and jumped astride of Manfred. She wasn't a small woman and Manfred gave a cough and the kitten popped out. It was a little wet but unharmed. Manfred didn't mean harm; he was just playing with it.

She took the kitten back to the pet store and, yes, they would take it but couldn't give any of her money back. When she got home, Manfred had done a little wrecking job. Not intentionally, but every time he turned around or wagged his tail, a lamp would go over – or a chair upset.

When Bill Frank came home that night, Mighty Manfred was waiting for him in his back yard. Bill finally had to take him back to the kennel in Michigan and give him back – for free.

Other Canine Acquaintances

There were scores of dogs with interesting behavior and many with ironic fates. There was the dachshund brought to me with an advanced case of distemper. He hadn't been vaccinated for the disease and hadn't eaten for many days. He could hardly walk, having the advanced stage of hardpad disease. I had never seen one to recover and recommended that for humane reasons that the dog be euthanized. The owner didn't want that so I treated the dog to my best ability and sent him home. A week later the dog was returned, very emaciated and in worse condition. The owner still wanted him treated so I did. I didn't see the dog for several weeks and then the owner brought him in: this time for a rabies shot and the dog unbelievably was almost recovered. He was eating, gaining weight and the hard pads had peeled and new soft skin allowed him to walk. The irony was that two days later the dog was so well that it ran out in the road and was killed by a car.

Then there was Watsie Shere's coonhound Dum Dum. Watsie loved animals of all kinds and had a pet squirrel he befriended when the squirrel showed up with a metal collar, having got it stuck while rummaging in the garbage. He also had a chicken that he got for his children at Easter when it was still legal for pet stores to sell dyed chickens. This chicken grew up to be an arrogant big cockerel so the city police forced him to take the cock to a farm. The cock not only terrorized the dogs and cats in the neighborhood, but on a few occasions took on human passersby strolling down Washington Street.

Watsie was musical and when he brought Dum Dum in to my office, he would show off his dog by whistling or humming a tune, and Dum Dum would go into his dance. He would prance around lifting his front feet high, whirling around to the time of the music. The dog got its name because he never learned how to go down stair steps. He had no trouble going up the stairs, but someone had to carry him down. Watsie had enough of that so he ordered the dog down and gave him a push. The dog slid all the way down. Thereafter the dog had no trouble. When he was ready to go down, he just doubled up his legs and slid all the way.

Near the end of my practice years there was a blonde cocker I clipped two or three times. The first time I was in the office in the evening, and this chap stopped in to see if I would clip the dog. Now I ordinarily did little or no grooming or boarding because I didn't have the time. My large animal or farm practice was usually a long day's work and during busy times, especially in the spring, my working day was often twelve to sixteen hours. Sick, accident or emergency calls were handled when they occurred, but pet practice that was routine was ordinarily taken care of during the noon hour or in the evening.

Well, I accepted the chore of clipping the dog since he was there; and then the owner informed me that the dog would have to be anesthetized. He would throw a fit

Other Canine Acquaintances

when he heard the clippers. Hearing this I told the owner to go into the waiting room out of sight and with a firm grip on the collar, I started the clippers a distance from the dog, then brought them closer. Talking to the dog, I clipped him completely and he didn't quiver or move a muscle. The owner was astounded. My monologue to the dog was low enough so the owner couldn't understand. It probably was something like this: "Listen my blonde friend. I'm your pal and if you don't move too much, I probably won't cut off either ear, but if you try to bite, I'm likely to bop you over the head with clippers so stay put."

Well, some six months later this man called me again and asked could he bring the cocker in for another clip. It was my busy season so I told him I just didn't have the time. He insisted that he would wait until I did have time as I was the only one the cocker would allow this job. He called the next evening, and I believe it was the third evening when he called I said, "Okay. Bring the dog in at 10 p.m. I'll have time then."

He did so and again I and the dog got along just fine. Some forty-five minutes later the job was finished. When the chap left he gave me these serious pearls of wisdom: "Doc, you've got to slow down. You can't work until 11 p.m. and keep your health. Life is too short! You're burning the candle at both ends."

I replied, after I regained my composure, "Oh, this isn't too hard on me. I enjoy a good chat with my doggy friends. Your dog and I understand each other perfectly!"

The Horned Animal

Inasmuch as my experience with the moose, the musk ox and the unicorn was of the very minimum in my large animal practice, my dealing with horned animals was almost exclusively with the bovines.

Of course horns or antlers in the wild animals served to some extent as a means of defense. This purpose is largely unnecessary in the domesticated animals. Of course certain breeds of cattle are "polled" or lacking in horns. The Angus is a notable example. Without going into detail about the means of defense in either wild or domestic animals – I would mention that in domestic animals on the farm, if "hooking" or "butting" is not effective or dangerous, kicking is sometimes substituted.

Such is the situation with the Angus. This skill is rather well developed. There are those who claim that an Angus can kick a fly off his ear with his hind legs. I think this is an exaggeration. It may have been Dr. Hayer who made that claim. When I started practice, Dr. Hayer was the McLean county veterinarian. His primary job at that time was TB testing in cattle. The procedure was to inject tuberculin into the caudal fold under the tail, so naturally he was prejudiced. I was assisting him on one occasion with a herd of Angus. Now Dr. Hayer was a Christian gentleman, an elder and lay preacher with his

The Horned Animal

church and never used profane or uncouth language; nevertheless, after receiving a half dozen juicy kicks to various parts of his anatomy, I distinctly heard him mutter, "The good Lord never made many mistakes, but he miscalculated when he perfected the Angus."

Of course here I am not exposing the kickers – but dealing with the horned animal. The most spectacular of the horned bovines is, naturally, the Texas longhorn. It was almost a wild animal and well-adapted to its environment. Unlike the better quality beef, it was resistant to the ticks, to cattle fever, to heat and its magnificent six foot horns was a menace to cougars, coyotes and other predators. It was also slim, fast and agile. This, of course, was the animal that made up the famous trail herds from Texas to Dodge City or Abilene in the nineteenth century. It was never prime beef and never dehorned.

Today in many places one might see mounted polished six-foot horns of the longhorn. The cost of this display is probably ten times what the whole animal would have brought at the rail-head in Dodge in the last century. In cross-breeding and in other improvements, the Longhorn has been displaced, but a few still flourish as hobbies.

In the Corn Belt, horns in cattle were just a nuisance. Certain breeders of purebred cattle keep the horns on their herds for show and identification. To neutralize the hazards, they attach iron weights to the tips and as they develop, the horns grow downward and inward. Identification can be burned painlessly on these horns. On a few occasions I have had to nip off a few inches of the tips when they have pierced or threatened to pierce the cow's head. This procedure lessens the havoc of the horns on their fellow animals as well as the hazard to humans.

For anyone not in the purebred business it was quicker, easier and cheaper just to call the veterinarian and get the horns whacked off, the bleeding arrested and the animal released to go back on feed without a setback. Dehorning was a significant part of my practice. It began in the fall, after the first frost and after the fly and maggot season ended, and usually terminated in March before fly season. It was heavy work: catching the animal in my chute, immobilizing the head and using the Texas dehorners (about twenty pounds in weight) to snip through two or three inches of skin, horn and bone and then stop the bleeding with forceps and dust the wound. I slept well after running fifty or sixty head through my chute.

But why dehorn?

I received a call on a sick steer located on the Adlai Stevenson farm. This steer weighed perhaps seven hundred pounds and had about ten inches of pointed horn on either side. He had pneumonia. At that time my best remedy for pneumonia was a sulfa drug given intravenously. I secured the steer's head in the care of the tenant owner and put a sixteen gauge needle into the jugular vein. The tenant seemed more interested in watching my procedure than in holding the head firm and the steer jerked his head around and drove his left horn into my right eye. I thought I had lost my eye. I hadn't but I sure did have a two week shiner and a peeved attitude. Both the steer and I recovered. Had it been an Angus, he may have tried to kick me but he wouldn't have endangered my eye.

The Horned Animal

Actually, dehorning wasn't done just to protect veterinarians or even handlers. Primarily it was to protect other animals and for economic reasons. If the cattle feeder shipped a load of fat steers to market and they still had their horns, he likely would be severely docked. A buyer would not care to pay prime beef prices for several hundred pounds of largely useless horns; and he might suspect some bruised and damaged meat from intramural horseplay among the herd.

Lloyd Boitnott, one of my clients near Carlock, decided to go into dairying. He bought a small herd of Guernseys, all of which still had their horns. The previous owner kept them stanchion most of the time with little or no freedom. Lloyd turned them out for exercise and comfort and for two days he got little milk as these animals battled to establish their place in the pecking order. When Lloyd called me to treat one for mastitis from bruises to the udder, I suggested dehorning. He declined saying that would probably be so hard on them; they might all dry up.

Two days later Lloyd called me to see if I could get up there that afternoon to dehorn the herd. He had just pulled a Guernsey out of his large water tank where she had been deposited by some of the others; he wanted all the horns off immediately. He later reported his milk production was up – even that evening right after the dehorning.

Then there was this client up by Lake Bloomington. His name was Les Smith and was a good client. Most of my calls there were on the quarter horses, but he did have a small herd of milk cows. He called me to come for dehorning his cows.

I pulled my chute those fifteen miles for his job. Since he was only milking about a dozen cows, it wasn't a long chore. As I was jacking up my chute for the return home, I saw an old cow plodding up the lane toward the barn. I said, "Hey Smitty, you overlooked one cow or is that the neighbor's?

"No," he said. "That's my old Bessie. She's a gentle old gal and never uses her horns; in fact, all the rest pick on her."

Well I returned home and something like three or four days later I got a call from Smith. He said, "Doc, I guess you've got to come back. Old Bessie has completely changed her disposition. Now she's hooking and butting all the other cows all over the place." I had to hitch up my chute and pull it those fifteen miles just to dehorn one cow.

I've never made a serious study of the philosophy or psychology of animals, but over the years in my dealings with them, I have amassed some understanding. Animal behavior in the dumb beast is almost as interesting as the animal behavior of their owners. Old Bessie wasn't exactly a Dr. Jekyll and Mr. Hyde but her indignities of long standing were for a glorious four days most fully revenged. I never checked with Smitty on how the pecking order stacked up afterwards. Whether Old Bessie retained her number one status or reverted back to her lowly stage, I don't know, but the lack of horns would have surely made the order a little more humane.

Euthanasia

The temptation to compare the art, the science and the surgery of the veterinarian to that of the human practitioner is, of course, rather ridiculous; although, parallels and similarities do exist. It is enough to say the doctor of human medicine deal only in one species of animal − Homo-sapiens − while the general veterinary practitioner may deal with a dozen species or sub-species. Further, the doctor of humans, in this age, usually deals with one area of the human body and probably only with a specific age group.

On one long, varied day I set a record for myself by calling on to treat beef cattle, dairy cows, horses, swine, sheep, goats, chickens, dogs, cats, and parakeets. Of course that was exceptional. Nevertheless each species was different, had different tolerances, anatomy and physiology. As an example, if you wished to allay pain or dull action in a dog you could give him morphine. If you gave morphine to a race horse, he would run faster − though you might be barred from the track. If you gave it to a cat, you would have to remove it from the ceiling.

I would add that I never gave morphine to any animal. I never had a license for any of the opiates, didn't purchase a safe to keep them in or bother with the paperwork or the hazards of being broken into for such drugs.

Some of the points I am endeavoring to stress are: firstly- the doctor of humans has technology, procedures, facilities and equipment not perfected or economically available to the veterinarian. Secondly, costs do not enter in. Thirdly, he can converse and pose questions to his patient and finally, he has only one aim and this curing, easing and prolonging life.

The veterinarian, on the other hand, can't converse with his patient – with the possible exception of the myna bird, and it would probably lie anyway. Also the large animal or farm practitioner is usually called for economic reasons, more often than humanitarian. He is not likely to be called for a sick sheep worth eight dollars if the veterinary charge is ten dollars. It would be different if several animals or whole flocks were threatened.

In that respect, the small animal or pet practitioner is more allied to the doctors of the human animal. Relatively few of the pets have resale value or economic significance. Their value lies in the regard their master holds for them. Yes, they are part of the family.

The veterinarian does have one recourse not available to the doctor of humans. He can use euthanasia if the animal owner requests it and he deems it proper. Humane laws do exist, but the animal is property and may be disposed of at the owner's whim. This humane procedure then is one advantage we hold for the terminally ill, the living but vegetative animal and the dangerous animal.

Frances Elfstrand was a very nice lady. She was an attorney and when she first came to me, she brought her fourteen year old cocker spaniel. This dog was deaf, blind, obese, almost completely inactive and incontinent. Of course the odor, wet fur and flushed skin was obvious. Frances then said, "Doctor, I know what you will recommend but she is like family to me. I just can't face putting her down." She then added, "Can you help her?"

I replied, "Yes, I can give here a shot that will help her retain her urine. It will last only a few weeks or so and can be given again but the interval will be shorter each time." I continued, "Yes, she is one of your family but is no long a pleasure but a burden to you. You can keep her until she finally expires. I would suggest that when you are convinced that she no longer has any pleasure in herself, in you or her existence, you will be ready to do the humane thing."

About a month afterwards I gave the dog a second shot but after a couple of weeks, Frances brought her back and said, "I don't know why I should be so emotional, but I'm resolved. I wouldn't wish to prolong my own life under similar circumstances so I'm ready to do the kind thing for my pet."

In contrast was another call I received from a woman who lived on the west side of town. I never knew her but she asked if I would come to her house to put her cat to sleep. She said it was old and sick but she had no means of bringing it to my office. When I agreed, she gave her address but added, "Don't park in front of my house. I live on a corner so park on the side street near my back door and come in that way."

Well, I followed her directions, somewhat mystified and when I got to her back door, she was waiting and hustled me inside. She then suggested that I not show myself near the front door as her nosey neighbor kept an eye on her. Sure enough, I peeked through the front door and across the street, behind a screened door, a woman sat on a rocking chair surveying the house I was in. With my inquiring look, my hostess with her toothless bright smile stated, "We don't get along. When this stray cat came along, I took it in and fed it but she claims it was once her cat. She hasn't had a cat for years so is trying to make trouble."

Then with her vivacious grin she said, "I think we should go out the back door and drive around Miller Park for awhile until she gets tired of staring out that door."

I then inquired, "Where is this cat and what's wrong with it?"

"I'm afraid it's got TB," she replied. She opened another door and a young, sleek black cat strolled out and friendly-like arched its back and rubbed against my leg.

I considered making a run for it but instead pulled out my stethoscope, pretended to listen to various organs, peered into the cat's mouth, eyes and ears then pronounced, "No, there are no symptoms of TB or other disease. Ethics will not allow me to destroy it." I ducked out the back door and didn't bother to present a bill for my professional services.

I don't really know how many animals I had to euthanize during my practice years - not too many as I recall and all for legitimate reasons. It was never on my conscience to destroy the dangerous or vicious animal nor did it bother me to terminate animals for humane reasons. The cases mentioned are but a sample, but I will mention one more.

Euthanasia

A year or so after the black cat episode, I got a call from a woman who wished for me to put down her old helpless dog. She lived in the north part of town on the second floor of a converted apartment; she had no means of transport. I agree to come.

I climbed the steps and rapped on the door. The door opened and I was stunned to see a small healthy dog in the arms of her with the broad, toothless smile. I could never forget it. I blurted out, "I still don't put the healthy friendly animal to sleep." I quickly went down the steps without waiting for the proposal of a friendly jaunt around Miller Park.

Golf

Throughout my memoirs I have mentioned my experiences with athletics and sports. In addition to the sports played at various schools, I did play a little sandlot baseball and played softball in both the Danvers and Carlock leagues as a catcher. I even came out for track in high school after baseball was eliminated. Hap Ahrends decided my legs were in best shape, and he had me running the mile since he had no good distance runners. The only school's miler I beat was Bloomington High; very few points were won by me but I was on the team. Now that pretty well describes my athletic experiences. I was always on the team but never a star.

Of course there were other sports. I learned tennis at Wapella and played quite a bit at Cassoday since there were no golf courses around. I won a first place medal in horseshoes in intramurals at Kansas State but water sports were completely missed by me. There were no swimming holes deeper than two feet while I was growing up so swimming, diving and winter ice skating was and is about as foreign as Latin.

But this discussion is on golf. I guess I should say something philosophical about golf. It has to be one of the dumbest games. You hit a little ball then carry, pull

Golf

or tote thirty or forty pounds of largely unused or unnecessary equipment from one to two hundred yards to where the ball is and repeat the process. This is unless it, the little white ball, suddenly curves one way or the other seeking shade in the timber or cunningly snuggles down under rank grass or thorny brush. Then it more resembles the childish game of hide-the-thimble. The manufacturer of these balls has some secret process or ingredient that causes them to be shade and water lovers. The little ball never passes a chance for a cool dip in nearby streams or settles under vegetation.

Of course it is supposed to be a game for older citizens to get exercise out in the open spaces on pristine green fairways or shaded avenues of oaks or pines. Then, of course, they invented electric golf carts so they only physical exertion is stepping in and out of the cart and making an occasional swing with one of the twelve or fourteen clubs you have to invest in.

Now, of course, most clubs and public courses require you not only to pay a green fee of about twenty dollars a round but most require a golf cart which will require another twenty dollar rental. Of course if you are allowed to own your own cart (which cost about the same as a good used car) they have trail fees for you to use your own cart. This will come to from five hundred dollars to six hundred dollars per year. Then you have an additional cost – you have to join the Y.M.C.A. to get the workout these extra costly amenities have cheated you out of.

If you are a "scratch" player and play twice a week, own your own cart, invested in a complete set of clubs and two dollar golf balls, have all the proper apparel and manage not to break too many windows, it will cost you about fifty cents for every swing of the club. Or in other words, about forty dollars per round. That's ten dollars per hour for all that fresh air, beautiful scenery, vigorous exercise and pristine flora – if you stay out of the poison ivy – doctor bills not included.

But the system can be beaten. If you have just discovered golf and play every day, two rounds on some days – and your handicap is thirty six or forty, it reduces the cost of each swing down to about six cents.

It is surprising that I still play golf. When I started the game, I could check out a set of clubs from the athletic department at ISU, buy golf balls for twenty two cents (new) and play eighteen holes at Highland for fifteen cents. My first set of clubs I owned cost me five dollars, including the bag. I got it from a pawn shop.

Of course it doesn't cost me fifty cents a swing. My handicap has gone up to where I get a lot more swings for my money. The fresh air and the pastoral setting are still there and though Shockey is no longer around, the congenial fellowship abounds and your opponent is yourself and the course.

Yes, golf is mysterious. As Barth said one time when we were playing Highland in July with the temperature ninety five degrees and he was finishing a horrendous hole- something like an eight on a par four – wiping the perspiration from his brow, "And my wife thinks I'm out here having fun!"

George Burns, commenting on the old saw about getting out of bed on the wrong side, "I don't care which side I get out. At my age, I'm just happy to get out of bed."

As I said before; sure it's a stupid game but I enjoy it because I can still get out of bed and swing at that little white ball.

I guess I played my first game of golf when I was a senior in high school. I remember I took sixty-one strokes to negotiate the first nine holes. The second nine I lopped off ten strokes and took a fifty-one. I never took lessons but decided it was an easy game and never intended to take over fifty strokes for nine holes thereafter. I don't think I ever did for nearly sixty years, but golf is a game for any age, and lately a fifty is not all that foreign to me.

Carolyn and Paul O'Brien

Golf can be described in many ways, but for me it was the proper sport for the large animal veterinarian. That is because it is usually indulged in on warm sunny dry days. During the busy season for farmers, they are reluctant to leave the fields to call a veterinarian. If they have an emergency, it is usually discovered early in the morning, or if less pressing, it can be postponed until darkness takes them from their planting or harvest. That leaves the veterinarian with little to do during the middle of the day. If rain keeps them out of the field, they may think of numerous chores that needs a veterinarian. But then if it is raining, the veterinarian can't play golf anyway.

For that reason, I usually planned on playing golf on Thursday afternoons. O'Brien was a drug salesman for Norden Laboratories. He knew that I could usually be found in my office around noon, and he played a few rounds with me at Highland Park. One Thursday my daughter Carolyn who was in high school said, "Dad, how about letting me play golf with you today?"

I said, "Sure, why not?" I didn't have any conflict.

About that time O'Brien showed up and he said, "Doc, I've got my clubs with me, and I'd like to go out and win back some of those nickels."

Now I have never wished to play for big money and always insisted on nickel or dime games. It is a much more fun game, nobody loses much and one can chide someone on a lousy shot with no one losing his temper or splitting up friendships.

When I said fine to O'Brien, Carolyn said rather sadly, "Does that mean I can't play?"

I reassured her she was welcome to play.

O'Brien then said, "I'll be ready to go in about forty-five minutes; I have to call on Dr. Wainscott first."

I suggested that he call Wainscott and maybe he could play, and Paul could take his drug orders out at Highland. He did so and Don said he wasn't too busy and would meet us at the course. Of course Carolyn then wistfully asked, "Does that mean I can't play?"

Again I replied, "Of course you can; there will just be four of us."

Well, on the first hole, I got a good drive right down the middle, and Carolyn, who is best with an audience, hit a dandy. O'Brien who was strong but a little erratic hit a big one, but with his frequent hook, put it in the creek at the left. Carolyn, with a bit of a smirk then said, "Mr. O'Brien, you and I are playing for a nickel also."

O'Brien then rather surprised said, "Oh, we are? Well OK."

Carolyn was on the green in two as I was. She took two putts for a par four and I made mine for a birdie. Paul after a penalty, hit over the green and got down with a six. Wainscott ended with a five or six, whereupon O'Brien said, "Doc, it's bad enough for you to trounce us but to bring your daughter out to beat us is downright humiliating.

Carolyn then said, "Mr. O'Brien, we pay off after every hole."

Paul surprised again said, "We do?" But he pulled out a nickel and handed it to her.

Carolyn pocketed the nickel and said, "Mr. O'Brien, that's the last hole we're playing for money!"

Harry Schockey

Harry was a great golfer. By that I don't mean he was extremely skillful. I could usually beat him by five or ten strokes, but he had the true golfing spirit. He rarely let business, poor health or weather interfere with his pursuit of the little white ball. He had an insurance agency and always claimed that he was following up insurance leads while on the golf course. Of course he had my business as well as Bill King's and Glen Mohr's; but he always wanted to be handy if someone might by chance take out another policy. He was the eternal optimist and always expected that the next round was going to be his greatest. If we were each off the green in three and our opponents were dead to the pin in two, he couldn't concede. He would say, "You don't know; we might sink our shot. They might miss their putt."

Yes, Harry had the true golfing spirit and thus was a great golfer.

He was the organizer, made up the games, arranged the partnerships and odds. After one round, I found that I was you might say "his permanent partner". Glen Mohr was about my speed and Bill King maybe slightly better than Harry but it was not one-sided. More often than not, there were other regulars: Jack McKay, Bill

Sullivan, Lou Rogers, Pete Schmidt, and Barth. No matter how many, Harry and I were partners, and we might have three or four nickel games going.

One time, Bill, Glen Harry and I went to Morton for the Normal "Town and Gown" play day. It was a terrifically hot day and we teed off near noon. I had never played the course, but I had one of my best days – the first nine that is. I had two birdies and four pars and came in one over par. We had Bill and Glen down something like seventeen points and each point represented a nickel. As I say, it was hot! Harry said, "Doc you've been playing terrific. I'm going to have an ice cold beer and I'm going to buy you one, too."

Well, that beer felt fine. About half way down, the starter called our foursome to tee off for the second nine and I had to chug-a-lug the rest of the beer. When I teed off, I had a little problem figuring which of the little white balls I should try to hit. I settled on the middle one and managed to dribble it about fifty yards down the hill. With Harry voicing constant disapproval, I managed an eight on that par four hole. Three or four holes went by before I could concentrate on just one ball, and by that time our insurmountable lead had shrunk to six points. I then got a couple of pars and we came out about twelve points ahead, but Harry never forgave or forgot my collapse. Many times afterward he mentioned that he would never buy me another beer unless by chance I became his opponent.

Harry was a man of many words and used them frequently. Since he played football at Bloomington High when I was playing for NCHS, he always assumed we were about the same age. When he found out that I was more than two years older than he, he never let me forget. One time when he was retelling for the fourth or fifth time the golf story about the fellow taking off his hat when the funeral procession for his wife passed by, I interrupted him.

"Harry, since you have been carrying me all these years on the golf course, I expect you to be a pall bearer at my funeral. You just as well carry me at the end. However, I will leave instructions to be sure that my funeral will not be held on a Thursday because I couldn't get you off the course that day unless we were on tornado watch or in a blizzard."

Ironically some fifteen years ago, the situation was reversed. It was the first warm days of spring; I stopped by Harry's office to see how he was feeling. He had had two moderate to severe heart attacks but recovered to resume golf. Once when he was recovering but still not up to playing, I hired a cart for him to ride along. We told him we had to have him to arrange for the games and needed his advice and instruction as we were constantly at a loss on our own. When he did play, I usually pulled his cart and clubs up the steeper hills.

On this April day, he said he felt fine and was raring to go. This was the first game of the season, and I think we had some eight or ten of the regulars which, of course, Harry proceeded to pair up – all against McCannon/Schockey.

Well, Harry played well and after twelve holes, we had a substantial lead over all pairs. He was in the group behind me and after I parred the thirteenth, I looked around and said, "If Harry makes it over the lake, we can limp in."

Well, he carried the lake and I teed off on the fourteenth. I got to my ball and there were the fellows behind shouting. Sullivan was shouting, "Harry's down." Before the paramedics got him to the hospital, he had paced off his last putt. I was sure of it when I called Marie his wife. Marie met us at the hospital with the sad news. We were shocked and unprepared to console Marie, but she proceeded to console us. Dry-eyed she said, "Boys, don't feel too sad for Harry. The time had come, and he went the way he would have chosen. He was doing just what he most liked: playing golf on a beautiful spring day among his friends. It is a beautiful way to go."

Well, we were the pall-bearers and we didn't get over mourning for some time. I couldn't play for a couple of weeks. When we did gather on the first tee finally, we must have looked confused. Bernie Seltzer yelled over from the tenth tee, "What's the matter with you guys? Don't you know how to start a game when Harry's not with you?"

On Leaving Private Practice

I never had a salaried job until I was graduated from Illinois State Normal University in 1938. Few farm boys had paying jobs since work on the farm took all summer, evenings and vacation time. I worked for the Weather Bureau for about two and one half years then with the Civil Aeronautics Administration for eight years before resigning in January 1948 to go back to Kansas State University to get my veterinary degree in 1953. I started my practice at Bloomington, Illinois and was in General Practice for fifteen years.

My practice years were happy and productive; although I started at the advanced age of thirty-eight. (I still wasn't the oldest in my class.) These years possibly were the peak years for the family veterinarian of the small farm practice. Sulfa drugs came into use on farm animals early in my college years and penicillin was first used at KSU during my junior year. Livestock prices were good and the small farmer was moderately prosperous so he called on his veterinarian frequently. In 1958 and 1959 I had as clients some seventy-five farmers who sold milk, and during this time I vaccinated each year as many as seventeen thousand pigs for cholera and erysipelas.

However in 1967, Dr. Clarno the County Veterinarian died. Sometime later a few of the County Supervisors inquired if I was interested in the position. I didn't think I was but a few months later I reconsidered. Hog cholera vaccine was about to be banned; farms were becoming consolidated leaving fewer small operators and less and less animals. Where once I had seventy-five dairy clients these had disappeared down to twenty-five and only horse practice was on the increase.

A steady job with fewer hours began to look more interesting. I was fifteen yeas older, and the allure of the midnight obstetric call in January was not as glamorous as it was in my younger years.

Well, I applied for the job and was selected. Dr. Little took over my practice and I took over a different career. My new job was to test and eliminate TB and brucellosis in cattle, be responsible for sanitation and inspection of sales barns and to inspect and bring slaughtering plants up to state standards. I was also to be Rabies Control Officer and supervise the county animal shelter. This was to be all within McLean Country.

In six months my county was certified TB and brucellosis free, the two meat plants came up to federal standards so the state decided we no longer needed a county veterinarian. The state was paying all my expenses and half my salary and the county the other half. They were involved in bringing all meat plants up to federal standards and so wanted me to work entirely for the state as District Meat Inspector for some seven counties from Kankakee to Urbana and west to Woodford County. Now I had no idea that the county would pick up my entire salary so I opened negotiations

On Leaving Private Practice

with the state veterinarian. They were to send me to a federal inspected meat plant for training that would take from six weeks to three months.

Since this job would begin in January, I inquired where they would send me and their answer was St. Paul, Minnesota. No way would I go there for a winter vacation so they offered Omaha. That might be a slight bit better, but it still wasn't warm enough so they called Washington and got permission for me to train at Ft. Worth so that was better.

While I was talking with Springfield, the County Supervisors met and decided they could afford to hire me full time without state support so I never became a meat inspection supervisor. I became County Veterinarian and Animal Control Administrator for McLean County.

Animal Control

To summarize animal control before describing any of my experiences would be to classify it as an impossible job to please more than a small percentage of people even when doing a correct and reasonable activity. You can see that there are so many classes of animals, so much difference in size and disposition among the same class of animals. And among people there are those too tolerant and feel no control is necessary, and those of the opposite belief: that animals should never have public freedom or should be eliminated.

Among most people, however, their tolerance extends to a few species and intolerance applies to a few species. To demonstrate this, one morning I received a call from an irate lady who said, "Doctor, I wish you would pick up and destroy the cats in my neighborhood. The owners let them out and they stalk birds. We would like to have songbirds next in our trees and shrubbery and these cats try to catch them all the time."

Before the day was over, I received another call from a second irate lady who stated, "Doctor, I wish you would do something about the blackbirds in my back yard. I've got a cat and every time I let it out, these birds dive on it and chase it back into my garage. They are making a nervous wreck of my cat!"

Even among the same species, particularly dogs, there is the same conflict. The owners of the small dogs (Pekes, Chihuahua) demanded confinement for large dogs while the owners of German shepherds, boxers say "Dogs will be dogs. Let them take care of themselves."

An exception was Joe Schneider's dachshund Duchess. She took an intense dislike to a German shepherd down the street and when she was let out, she would dash across Fell Avenue and down the street and take on the shepherd. Joe would have to bring Duchess to me to be patched up after every encounter. He never blamed the shepherd and was never able to convince Duchess that if she couldn't adopt a more pacific attitude, she at least should choose an adversary more in keeping with her own size.

Wild animals brought on considerable number of complaints, but most were protected by wildlife laws so I didn't waste much time on any of them except the skunk. The skunk was the primary reservoir for rabies in our area and was taken off the protected list. Not that he needed protection because he could take care of himself, and a few did wander into town. During my twelve years of tenure as Rabies Control Officer, I don't believe any human was bitten by a skunk, no human died of rabies and very few had to take the post-exposure treatment. Those who took the treatment were mostly farmers or veterinarians who examined the mouth of cows who were sick and salivating excessively like they had something caught in their throat.

During the rabies epizootic of 1971-72, I sent in more than a hundred heads of suspects, most of which were skunk. One of those years we had seventy-two that tested positive at the state laboratory. We had one dog, one raccoon, one fox, one sheep and two bovines; and all the rest were in skunk.

Now as I said no one died of rabies in my country; actually no one died during those years from rabies in the entire United States. However, in 1971 I believe it was, two people died in Illinois of taking the post exposure treatment. They probably developed sensitivity to the treatment and went into shock during treatment. The irony of it was that they may not have been exposed and likely were bitten by an animal that could not be identified and caught. Any human exposed to the rabies virus had to take the treatment, as there has never been anyone with rabies recover; but if the biting animal is kept under observation for ten days and is still alive, it didn't have rabies at the time of the bite. Eight days was as long as any dog had been known to live after the virus reached his saliva.

With over a million animal bites each year in the USA and with humans, some twenty five thousand each year taking the treatment, one can see my problems in animal control. Dogs account for more than eighty percent of all bites in humans, but skunk account for more than eighty percent of the rabid animals. The dog had to be kept vaccinated, biting dogs had to be kept under observation and strays had to be kept at a minimum and away from skunk. I killed two rabid skunks with clubs but wouldn't have gone within twenty feet of a healthy one.

My experience with owners of unvaccinated biting dogs was fascinating but definitely a nervous vocation. Willie Pate caused more than his share of problems

Animal Control

although he didn't alarm me too much. On one occasion the city police contacted me after a bite and asked if I wanted an officer to accompany me to Willie's house. I inquired if he was that troublesome and they informed me that he wasn't too bad when he was sober. On further inquiry they said he was sober nearly half the time. Later I found that was the time he was in jail since he divided his time about equally between home and jail.

I declined the police offer and called on Willie that evening. I had to kick aside the whiskey bottles when he invited me in and found him watching TV on the one set that was still working. There were three or four other sets in the room, all with their glass fronts smashed. He apparently was a TV critic and expressed his displeasure by throwing empty bottles at programs that didn't come up to his standards. I don't know how he acquired so many sets. I didn't ask!

Well, I got his dog; kept it under observation for the required time, vaccinated it and got it registered. I had to keep it a few days extra as I had to use a little coercion to collect the cost from him for the county. He of course earned no wages, but his wife worked as a chambermaid and was the source of his funds. The day he redeemed his dog she wore a black eye – not too easy for a black woman. I felt badly for her and his family, but I figured that the larger losers were the stores where he bought his gin.

On another occasion of a reported bite, I had to call on a woman in the same part of town. She supposedly lived alone but when I was invited in, I thought I had blundered into a huddle of the offensive line of the Los Angeles Rams. They all seemed to me to be about seven feet tall and weighed about 285 pounds. At a later time, I thought in the surprise of the moment, I may have misjudged the stature and avoirdupois of this leather jacketed group – and yes, I was nervous indeed. Nothing happened; my business was transacted. The rather large gentlemen spoke not a word and almost all of them stared out the windows or faced other directions than where I stood.

Since skin color was mentioned in the previous paragraphs, I wish to pause here to disclaim any racial prejudice on my part – or at least I hope that I was reasonably free of such stigma. During my practice years, I had some dealings with the black population although we did not have a large black population in our town. Carroll Roundfield had two dogs and was a good client of mine over the years. There was a man named Thomas that ran a body shop and had a very fine home with a little acreage west of town and had called me from time to time on animal problems.

Then there was Buzz Thomas that ran a car body shop. I had employed him to work on cars for me and while he lived in town, he had a little acreage up near Carlock. He called me there a time or two on his pigs. One curious thing about Buzz, he seemed to have numerous female cousins. He introduced a new one every trip I made to his Carlock home.

Mrs. Carter was a large black lady with red hair and was a frequent client. On one trip she was thumbing through some of the magazines in my office and asked if I had a supply of old magazines. I told her my garage was stacked with them. She asked if she could have some of them as her boys liked to look at them. I filled her trunk with *Life, Look, The Saturday Evening Post,* and *The Readers Digest.* On another trip she had a cute little boy of about five with her; when my wife asked him his name, he answered "Wichard Pwyor".

I said, "You don't mean...?"

"Yes," she said, "His father is Richard Pryor. He is my nephew and mighty fine chap, even if I am his aunt."

At this my wife gave out a non-committal "Really" since she didn't know who Richard Pryor was. I did, however, since he had made his debut as a television comic, and he was on his way toward becoming a film star. Mrs. Carter stated Pryor was returning to Peoria for a visit and she would bring him over to meet us, but not to make any fuss – just have a bit of coffee and cookies and a few friends in that might want to meet him. Actually he never showed up although I immediately made know to my wife who Richard Pryor was.

On subsequent calls Mrs. Carter brought young friends with her. Chic, good looking young ladies dressed in the latest fashion: high heels with rhinestone sequins on shoes and one even with a blonde wig. They also had dogs, poodles beautifully trimmed with rhinestone collars.

A few days later Carroll Roundfield brought his dogs in. Now I didn't know Mr. Carter's name. She had told me, but with her cross between a Southern and New England dialect, I never really understood. I asked Carroll if he knew this rather large black lady with red hair, walked with a slight limp and drove an Oldsmobile of recent vintage. "Oh," he said. "You must mean Mrs. Cotta."

"Yes," I replied. Mrs. Carter comes here a lot with different people, and I was wondering about her."

"Well, don't worry about her Doc," he said. "She is a fine lady, honest and she won't get you in any trouble.

She runs a good house down by the viaduct on Main Street and a couple others over around Peoria. Those girls change back and forth between Bloomington and Peoria."

Then I remembered those magazines: all with my name and address on labels on the back. I was advertised in all the houses of Ill-Fame between Bloomington and Peoria. I don't know if I got any business as a result, but I doubt if anyone would admit it. I kept hoping someone would mention having seen my magazines because I wanted to ask them how they found out about them.

Now I am skipping around a bit. I went back to my practice years for this last episode but now resume my rabies inspection experience. Probably the hairiest experience was with a biting dog belonging to a motorcycle gang.

I got word on a bite involving a girl in the Heyworth area who had driven up to the Merna area to visit a friend. She rather got lost so stopped at what she thought was a farm house to inquire directions. It happened that this was the headquarters for a motorcycle gang, the only one in McLean County. She didn't know it and neither did I. At any rate no one was at home, and when she got out of her car to go to the house, several dogs circled her, and one – a three legged one bit her rather severely.

When I was notified by the sheriff, I went to the place. Still no one was home, but the guilty dog was there and as disagreeable as ever. He didn't get a chance to bite me. When I found no one there, I drove down a road about a mile from there where a former client of mine lived. When he heard my inquiry as to the dog's

Animal Control

owner, and where I could find him, he said, "Doc, you go on home and forget about that dog."

I told him I couldn't do that. I couldn't subject a girl to the series of painful and somewhat dangerous shots just because I was afraid to confront the owner. He replied, "Well, you go back to town and be sure Sheriff King or some of his deputies go with you. The fellow runs a little shop on West Washington Street by the railroad and sells parts for cycles and automobiles although there is considerable question as to where he gets those things he sells." He went on to say this chap was the leader of the local gang and rode with the Grim Reapers out of Peoria.

All this was not a very soothing discourse, but I didn't ask for the Sheriff's help; he probably wouldn't have given it anyway. I simply breezed in to the dark interior of the shop and found the proprietor: bearded, black jacketed but alone. I didn't know enough about motorcycles to engage in any chit-chat so I took a firm line by telling him he was in certain trouble in violation of state rabies laws as well as county lease and dog registration laws. I described what had happened about the bite.

I explained to him that I didn't think it would be necessary to bring the law into this. If he would surrender his dog to me to keep under observation at the county shelter for ten days then I would vaccinate it and all the rest of his dogs. At the end of that time I would also register them with the county; all would be in the clear (including myself). I guess he thought I was a friend as he agreed. After ten days all was well and I actually collected some ninety-five dollars for the county. I think my casual mention of keeping away from the law was what appealed to him, and my ten days of nervous anxiety vanished.

Well, that was a little bit of what rabies control amounted to. We had reported to us probably an average of two bites each day. Peggy Gibson, my very capable animal warden, took care of many and quite a number of the owners of biting animals took them to their own veterinarians. But I still took care of the stickier cases. Peggy carried a tranquilizer gun but used it rarely. She and I used it on a disagreeable stray in Towanda and a biting dog near Hudson before he could disappear into a cornfield.

On one occasion a boy from the Soldiers and Sailors Orphanage was bitten by a large black dog. The boy knew what the dog looked like, what street he was on when it happened and even knew that the owners saw it happen as they called the dog back home when the attack happened.

The Warden combed the neighborhood, took the boy along the street and we advertised in the newspaper for the owner to be identified. There was no answer. The doctor that was responsible for the children wanted to start the series of shots, but I got him to postpone them for a day or two while I combed my records for anyone in that area that owned such a big black dog. Of course I found about a dozen that could have answered to the boy's description. I called on every owner and about the last one, I located the dog chained in a back building. The owner admitted there was an incident but didn't think the boy was bitten and anyway his dog was vaccinated.

Well, the boy got a reprieve. He didn't have to take the treatment.

Other Animal Complaints

Rabies control was probably the most important job connected to my position, but it was not the only one. I dissected hundreds of skunks, sent to the lab countless numbers of brain tissue and followed up on every animal bite. I was reasonably satisfied with our results. No one died of the disease in my county or from taking the treatment. Only some six or eight individuals were put through the treatment and they had been exposed. I know of no case where anyone went through the treatment unnecessarily although the boy mentioned in the chapter called Animal Control came close.

But since I was listed in the phone book as the Animal Control Administrator, my wife and I were the recipients of countless animal gripes. When a citizen called to say the woodchuck denned up along the Illinois Central right-of-way was eating up their entire green bean crop or the neighbor next door to me complained when the squirrels chewed holes in his awning, I could only offer sympathy. I couldn't destroy animals unless they were dangerous, and certainly not those protected by law.

I did call on an elderly couple and removed a raccoon from their chimney and helped get rid of a squirrel in an attic one time. I say one time because I showed him the hole under the eaves where the squirrel got in and suggested that he patch it. He didn't bother to do so, and in a few months called to say either that squirrel or a relative had gotten in again. I wished him "good luck".

Then there was the town of Weston on the north edge of the county. I had never been in Weston until I became Animal Control, and after that I spent far too much time there. It was a small unincorporated town, but a good percentage of the inhabitants were "collectors". They collected junk! Old cars covered a few lots, but one individual collected not only old cars, but junk and garbage.

The old cars were two or three deep close around his run-down house. On top of these he tossed up cardboard boxes of garbage, not only his own but also from his neighbors. He had a small flock of ducks and these spent their lives atop this man-made mountain or in the trees. The garbage was their livelihood. They rarely came down as he had two or three dogs that would catch the ducks if they did. I don't know why he wanted the ducks. I don't think he could catch any of them and they didn't multiply as I am sure the rats got any eggs that were laid.

A large grain elevator occupied the center of town so with unlimited food and a safe harbor, rats were numerous indeed. To top it off there was, so far as I could determine, only one cat in town and it was kept indoors. Because of all the cat-hating dogs in town, this one cat couldn't venture outdoors.

The first call I got from Weston was from a neighbor of Junk Mountain. She complained that his dog had killed some of her pullets. When I called on her, she was washing clothes with a washboard and tub on her back

Other Animal Complaints

porch. The back door was open and some of her chickens were wandering in and out. I refrained from asking her if the dogs came into her house after the chickens. I had a bit of trouble finding the dog owner and proprietor of the mountain as he was out collecting garbage. When I did find him, he finally promised to pay the woman a few dollars for the chickens. I think he was of the opinion that she should keep the chickens in her house like the one cat that lived across town.

The dogs in Weston were adequately taken care of and well housed. One dog involved in a bite we checked on lived in a 1939 Chevrolet sedan. I did not care if the people of Weston wanted to have lots of dogs and let them roam free so long as that was the wishes of the citizens and no excessive public problem was created. I didn't like the rat situation but that was more under the jurisdiction of the county health department, and they had been trying for years to close up that haven. They were unsuccessful as of that time since much of the trash and the collection process were in place long before laws regulating such procedures were in existence.

One of my last complaints from Weston came not too long before I resigned my position. It wasn't the cause of my resignation. I had reached the age and position where I was ready for retirement, anyway…

This woman called and said, "Doctor, when are you going to do something about these dogs up here? They are a hazard. They chase kids riding bicycles and yesterday a friend of mine came to my house and the dogs circled her car and wouldn't let her get out. She had to drive up to the elevator and have the men there chase the dogs home so she could get out of her car!"

I assured her we would take some action.

I contacted Peggy Gibson and said, "Peggy, it looks like the people of Weston are ready for some action on their dog problem. You will have to work that area and bring in a few."

The next day Peggy brought in eight dogs from Weston. There were nine in the pack but by the time she caught the eight, the last German shepherd had gone home and was sitting on its own back porch. Peggy couldn't invade private property to take a dog from its own home.

Well, the next day the owner of the eight dogs came into the shelter with fire in her eyes. She was still firing the verbal invectives heading for the cages where her dogs were when Taylor stopped her saying if you open that cage you will only add to the charges against you. He enumerated the state and local ordinances she was guilty of and finished by saying, "You can take those dogs home with you by paying forty-four dollars right now. If you do and they run in a pack again they will be picked up again and charges will mount!" She calmed down somewhat, paid her forty-four dollars and took her dogs home to Weston.

And now for the epitome of irony, the epitome of frustration with humans in the field of animal control: One week to a day later, I received a call from Weston. The same woman called who called me earlier. She said, "Doctor, when are you going to do something about these dogs in Weston?"

I said, "Don't tell me. Do you mean those dogs are roaming free again?"

"Oh, no," she replied. "They have been chained up in their own yard and that's not fair to the dogs!"

Aftermath

These pages cover many of my memories from the "Early age of nothing" to my retirement in 1980. In re-reading, I realize how much that I could have added, but this was intended as a vignette and not a complete biography. My life did not come to a skidding stop with my retirement, but recent years are in the realm of my grandchildren. They can remember and record these years as they see fit. It is their world now!

Not too much mention has been made of my immediate family, my many friends, my parents or my grandparents. I could not do justice to what they have all meant to me. It was not my intention to recount details, construct a diary or record a pedigree.

It was my intention merely to describe certain experiences that would picture what my life was like, over much of the Twentieth Century, on the prairies of the Midwest.

During this span, I have had fun. I have had love and I have had contentment. What I have not had – is regret! I have been most fortunate indeed. And as the "aftermath" keeps on aftermathing along, I can only marvel at the manifold blessings that has followed me all of my days!

Stories For My Grandchildren

Birthday Letter: August 1990

Our Dear Michael,

On the event of your sixteenth birthday, we certainly wish you the best regards on this date. Happy Birthday!

About fifty nine years ago I, too, was approaching my sixteenth birthday. I don't recall anything significant about that date, but I believe I was just entering high school under circumstances rather alien to that of your sixteenth natal date. There were a few similarities. Since all seven of my Mooreville classmates repeated the fifth grade because of certain mathematical deficiencies, I was of the age of our sophomores at Wapella High. Since I could whip all the boys at Mooreville, I had no problems with either the freshmen or sophomores at Wapella.

As I advised Samuel, Spud Kinder, Guilty Duncan and Liver Ives, all who had flunked algebra the previous year, ganged up on me when I arrived at Deatley's barn to stable my horse, Mary Legs. I had to surrender my algebra homework for them to copy. That was of no consequence and I was glad to keep them eligible for our basketball team.

Birthday Letter: August 1990

I wasn't allowed to come out for basketball since practice was after supper and Mary Legs could not be called on to carry me twice to and from Wapella, four and a half miles each way and still leave me time for chores and a small amount of homework. Dad relented in the spring since practice and baseball games followed school so I played third base on a pretty good high school team.

The next year I played basketball, as my cousin Roy, a senior, had a Model T he called "the Puddle-Jumper". It had no top or heater so Mary Legs would have been warmer on January nights, but sometimes I rode home with Kelly Bishop. He had a sedan with only two windows broken out.

Driver's education and driver's licenses did not exist in those days. They weren't required for horses or I would probably have qualified by first grade. For autos, only permission from parents was needed. Since my family had only one car and I had an older brother, I had to depend on my horses or other boys who did have access to Model T's.

Not always was parental permission forthcoming. One summer day when I was in third or fourth grade, my mother and I were visiting the Longbrakes when Chink assured me he could drive. Now Chink was a year or two older than I although we were both in the same grade; so I, of course, questioned this claim.

Model T's of that era were rather complicated to drive and especially to start since most did not have starters and had to be cranked by hand. If the spark was advanced too far there was frequently a backlash on the crank and many a broken arm resulted. But I misjudged Chink. He may never have grasped mathematics or history, but he knew machinery. He got the Model T cranked up and with little old me perched beside him on the open touring car we started up Maple Avenue. My mother looking out a window, screamed, "There goes Julius! (His given name) He's driving your car and my Charles is with him!"

Well that odyssey was without any problems. Chink drove to our house and showed his skill in backing and turning, and we made it back safely. I got a bit of a talking to by my mother, and of course Chink got his daily whipping – but that was routine with him.

This little episode wasn't when I was sixteen. I think I was only nine. But when I started to high school, Chink had permission to drive the family Model T, and I rode with him on agriculture field trips and many other events. In fact he was driving when we freshmen explored the Haunted House after an evening of basketball at DeWitt.

He was also the driver on a field trip to The Spring when we freshmen took the afternoon off to go swimming in Beyer Griffith's pond on a hot day in late April or early May. We were supposed to be back in school, but Paul Powers had a flat tire – no spare – and Chink convinced the Ag teacher the he could find a replacement tire. Well, he finally did but it took him about four hours, and the rest of us were sick and tired of that cold water before he

Birthday Letter: August 1990

completed his mission. I almost missed a baseball game with Kenny that evening but got back just in time.

Lawrence Wade was our coach, but he was also the principal and in his latter capacity he had most of us stay in school an extra thirty minutes for two or three days. That was possibly the only punishment Chink ever escaped in his life as he didn't go swimming and did spend the afternoon hunting a spare tire.

Well, in another fifty nine years you might have a few reminiscences of your own sixteenth birthday and may they be as happy as mine and as pleased as I am of my sixteen year olds on this happy occasion.

Grandpa

Your grandmother sends a check to go with your ball retrieving profits toward some needed project.

Lioness Episode

The reason that I'm not at all proud of either this or the deer event is that they demonstrate how foolish I have been during my veterinary career; neither was heroic or Horatio Alger-like nor turned out brilliantly successful. The lioness caesarian occurred on June 20, 1958.

The veterinary care of the zoo was almost non-existent since facilities for handling animals there was non-existent. The older doctor, whose office was across from Highland Park, was nominally the zoo veterinary. He wouldn't go near the lioness. Grover Kathover who was in charge called Brookfield Zoo and they said get some posterior pituitary into her and just wait. Nothing else to do.

Well, on Thursday Grover called me to come help. I wasn't even aware that they had a pregnant lioness on hand but arriving there, it was obvious bad news. She had a fetid discharge with maggots crawling in and out of her. She was still active and dangerous. I cobbled together a three foot stick with a syringe taped to one end filled with barbiturate. With John Bray, the zoo assistant, maneuvering a long iron rod to get her close enough, my syringe on a stick aimed for her abdomen. A few broken needles later she finally passed out.

Lioness Episode

Dick Streckfess was a *Pantagraph* reporter and here is his report:

MILLER PARK ZOO WAS CLOSED THURSDAY AS DELILAH, A SEVEN HUNDRED POUND LIONESS UNDERWENT A CAESARIAN OPERATION IN HER CAGE. WORKING BEFORE ZOOKEEPEERS, TWO NERVOUS MALE LIONS AND HIS NERVOUS WIFE, VETERINARAIN CHARLES MCCANNON TOOK A DEAD CUB FROM THE LIONESS IN AN OPERATION THAT LASTED HALF AN HOUR.

Of course I loaded her up with sulfonamide powder, destroyed all the maggots and gave her a long lasting penicillin.

Well, she slept for two days so obviously we got too much anesthesia in her system. At any rate on Sunday she had revived enough to go through the door to the outside cage. I and John Bray crawled out to her and I loaded her up with plenty of the long lasting penicillin and a pint of dextrose. I'm sure the crowd gawking at the two men in the lion cage was surprised that Miller Park had tame lions.

As I have said, the lack of restraint facilities and this being well before the coming of the tranquillizer guns, perhaps six weeks later I was called by Grover to autopsy Delilah. Her uterus was healed perfectly but she died of multiple abscesses of the kidney and liver. John Bray should have brought her over to my office for antibiotic shots every couple of days for about a month.

Of course I never sent a bill to the city of Bloomington or to Miller Park. But then, I never afterward had to pay any golf fees to play golf at Highland Park.

Excerpt from (Bloomington, Illinois) *Daily Pantagraph*

Panic Stricken Deer Dies after Spree in IWU Building

May 23, 1980
by Dan Craft

"It was a bizarre and unhappy animal story that unfolded Thursday night on the Illinois Wesleyan University campus.

IWU students were walking down a sidewalk in front of Sherff Hall about 6 p.m. when seemingly from out of nowhere lurched a young deer, bleeding and panic stricken.

The deer then jumped three or four feet over a large bush in front of the hall's north side, crashed through a thick plate-glass window and went on a wild spree through the building's first floor. A security guard was able to lock the frightened animal in a lecture hall, but not before it had thrashed about in a small computer room and attempted to throw itself through a second plate-glass window.

... For more than a half hour, university officials were not sure what to do. There was concern the deer, later identified as a 1 ½ year old buck, would panic again and run through a wall of windows on the lecture hall's south end.

Police attempted to locate someone in the county with a tranquillizer fun but were unsuccessful. According to McLean County Veterinarian Charles McCannon, a tranquillizer gun probably would have made no difference. 'In the condition the deer was, he was not likely to survive a tranquillizer anyway.'

McCannon, carrying nothing but a rope, entered the lecture hall, hoping he would be able to keep the deer from exhausting itself further.

McCannon threw a lasso around the animal's neck while it paced nervously in the classroom's front.' The deer was badly cut up from the glass. He had bled profusely. There really wasn't anything I could've done…Once it gets frightened, it simply goes berserk and loses its mind.' "

In a letter dated, May 19, 2005…concerning deer story

Well, I got three columns in the *Pantagraph*, and yes, I caught the deer with the first throw of my lasso, tied its feet together and hoisted it onto Peggy Gibson's pickup. She took it to the rural area, but it was a goner by the time she released it. I didn't have to do any cleanup at Wesleyan.

… A bit about the animal population in McLean County. As a youngster there were rumors of the timber wolf. I never saw one or knew of anyone who saw one. A coyote was shot where the Normal golf course is now, but no one saw any other since – that was 1936. Nobody ever saw a deer in McLean or DeWitt counties during these years until about the time we set up practice, at which time they spilled over southward from Wisconsin. The deer had it made to McLean County – lots of corn fields

Panic Stricken Deer Dies in IWU Building

for feed, no open season and no predators. Then the coyotes discovered the migration and followed.

Pete Trent, Mary Norma's husband, stopped in one day for me to identify the animal he shot and had in his truck. It was a coyote, yet Pete had never seen one. Two years later Pete and his hunting buddies shot twenty-five. I have seen deer herds of twelve to fifteen. They sometimes move in with cattle around the haystacks.

On an early spring the corn is planted and up high enough for the does to drop their fawns in the corn fields - so survival is high. In a late spring the corn is not high enough so the fawns are dropped in timber areas and the coyotes have easy pickings. Both species are now very common there. The red fox is scarce. Quail and pheasant along with rabbit have moved into town. The rural areas are the battlefields of the deer and coyotes.

However, lions are still scarce in central Illinois.

You might be curious about how Miller Park started its zoo. It began with an African male lion being captured in McLean County. A circus train had left Bloomington when a railway section worker found this newborn cub along the tracks. This worker was Kinder, grandfather of Spud and Virgil Kinder of my Wapella High school days. The lion was young enough for Kinder to bring it to Bloomington and Judge Ramseyer ruled that it was a wild animal and captured in the wild so it was his property. Kinder wasn't confidant that it would make a good house pet so he gave it to the park, and the zoo thus had its beginning.

Written in a letter to the Petersons on May 26, 2005

Cousins

With the passing of Loren Rolofson, I thought I would write a bit about my Rolofson cousins. I guess there were fifteen of them. One or two I never met and of course several were considerably older. Four of the males were nearly the same age. Loren was the youngest being a little bit younger than me by three years. He was the best all-around athlete of the four. Roy was the eldest by two years and thus "the Boss" who frequently got the rest in trouble.

One Sunday the family all met at the Whitney farm for dinner. After the meal Roy, Louie and I explored the creek. When we returned, Loren advised us that Uncle Bill took the men out to his watermelon patch where he harvested one or two for their post meal snack. Of course Roy was indignant and said we would treat ourselves with Loren leading us to the patch. Well, I had some trepidations since four boys tramping around the patch did considerable damage. We opened several melons without finding a ripe one.

The next day Grace and Bill Whitney came to our place to report the damage and advise stiff penalties.

Letter to the Petersons on May 26, 2005

They never called on Uncle Frank or Uncle Monte since they were older, but Ines was younger. If Fred and Ines exerted punishment that would suffice. My punishment? My mother said, "Was it Roy that suggested your raid?" With my affirmative, she just said, "You did wrong. Don't let anyone ever lead you into doing such damage." That was my punishment.

Earlier stories in my memoirs mention Roy but this discourse is on all the cousins. At an earlier age when we met on Sundays after seeing Tom Mix, Jack Hoxie or Hoot Gibson in a movie at the K-Theater, our Sunday game was Cowboys and Outlaws. Loren being the youngest was designated the "Bad" guy. In later years, Loren lamented about how on many a Sunday afternoon he spent most of the time locked in the cob house. He would be released just to be hunted down and locked up again.

Later in life the four cousins got together for golf a few times. One July 4 we went out to Highland at 8 a.m. On the second hole a thunderstorm came up so we crept under shrubbery until we got thoroughly soaked. We decided that since we were already soaking we just as well play in the rain. The sun came out and by the time we finished eighteen holes, our clothes were dry. So we decided to play another round. Leaving the course Loren said, "Stop the car. I was supposed to play with those fellas that just came in." He played another round.

Then there was the time when your mother and I had vacationed on the Rio Grande and Loren's family and the Glen Mohrs were vacationing at Hot Spring. Loren had told us to meet him there. On Sunday Glen and I went out to play golf. Loren went to church with the women but instructed us to rent a cart and he would

Stories For My Grandchildren

meet us after our round. We did so after eighteen holes, we played another eighteen holes with one of us riding and one walking. Loren was playing our best ball for a nickel a hole. I was playing fair golf at that time and after those eighteen holes, we had Loren down by six points. He then said, "We have to start around again. I can't quit owing you guys money." On our forty-second hole, he beat both of us so caught up. He allowed two tired guys to quit.

Loren was a real hunter. One season I think he shot about ninety cock pheasants in Illinois, Iowa and South Dakota. He liked for me to hunt with him since the Illinois limit was two cocks per day. Usually two shots and he had his limit. Then he would tell me, "Get ready. One will be taking off!" Sure enough a rooster would rise, I would fire and miss. Loren would shoot. As the bird tumbled down, Loren would say, "Great shot Charles. You got him".

Loren was one of the first in Clinton to own his own golf cart – saying his knees were bad and he had to ride. In November he would tramp three or four muddy miles over corn fields, hunting pheasants or quail. But on a warm sunny June on solid fairways he had to ride.

Well of the fifteen Rolofson cousins, only one remains... your tired old Dad.

McCannon Family Tree

Fred Elbert McCannon
(1891-1971)
married
Mary Ines Rolofson
(1891-1981)

Dean	Minnie	Charles Frederick	Dale	Richard
(d 1966)	(d 1994)	married	(d 1979)	(d 1983)
married	married	Olive M. Gardner	married	married
Mabel	Norman		Mary	Peggy
Perry	Sutter		Louise Stine	Gerloff
(d 1969)	(d 1982)		(d 1984)	(d 1994)
(4 children)	(3 children)		(2 children)	(4 children)

Carolyn Jean	Nancy Ruth
married	married
Charles Theodore Peterson Jr.	Stephen Barasch

| Charles Theodore, III (Ted) | Michael Gardner | Samuel Peleg married Jill deBeers | Sarah McCannon |

May McMillan

Index

Abels, 44, 60
Abels, Jimmy, 57, 58, 60
Alexander, Chester, 86
Arends, Hap, 67, 215
Armstrong, Mrs., 24, 30, 31, 32, 34
Baird, Bob, 195
Barasch, Nancy McCannon, 10, 130, Family Tree
Barasch, Samuel, 9, 243, Endorsements, Family Tree
Barasch, Sarah, 10, Endorsements, Family Tree
Barnes, Cedric, 122, 123
Barth, 18, 223
Bearden, 67
Beich, Bill, 193
Beich, Patty, 193
Best, Ned, 43
Best, Vachel, 43
Bishop, Buck, 86
Bishop, Kelly, 11, 16, 29, 30-34, 40, 44, 57, 58, 60, 81, 244
Bishop, Walter, 54, 79
Bloomington Canning Company, 72
Blue River Valley, Kansas, 135
Bohrer, Al, 61
Boitnoit, Lloyd, 208
Bray, John, 151, 247, 248
Brokaw, Charlie, 164+
Brown, Elizabeth Gardner, 115, 129
Carnahan, 136
Carter, Mrs., 233
Chamberlain, Bob, 94, 99, 109, 113, 117
Chamberlain, Wilt, 10

Index

Civil Aeronautics Administration, 128-130, 226
Clinton, Illinois, 51, 80
Cole, Stan, 187
Conway, Bill, 61
Cordiss, George, 74
Coveys, 54
Covey, Cecil, 80
Craven, Pop, 89
Crum, Bert, 79
Davis, David, 26, 72
Deatley's barn(Wapella, Illinois), 243
Devine, Francis, 148
Douglas, Stephen A., 12
Duncan, Guilty, 60, 243
Elfstrand, Frances, 211
Flocken, Fred, 93, 109
Foley, Nate, 54
Fox, Albert, 83
Frank, Bill, 200
Frank, Jack, 137
Frazer, Evan, 59
Garrison, Kansas, 133, 134, 137
George, Jim, 60
Gibson, Peggy, 237, 241, 250
Gillis, Bob, 171
Gillis, Jack, 171, 173
Gillis, Ruel, 171, 173
Glunt, Orel, 135, 136
Green Mill Café (Bloomington, Illinois), 196
Greens 44, 60

Index

Green, Wilson, 22
Griffin, Babe, 68
Griffith, Beyer, 245
Grim Reapers Motorcycle Gang, 236
Gutherie, Lain, 94, 105
Hales, 16, 36
Hale, Arch, 52, 53
Hale, Wilma, 36
Harrison, Mr., 72
Harsh, Turk, 126
Harvey, John, 101
Head, Ed, 10
Heidelberg School (DeWitt County, Illinois), 26, 56
Hickman, Burl, 53, 54, 80
Hilger, Paul, 129
Hill, Gene, 87
Hines, Becky, 187
Hines, Don, 187
Hitch, Lou, 10
Hoffman, Red, 62
Hopkins, Jack, 76, 89
Illinois Wesleyan University, 250, 251
Kathover, Grover, 247
Irish Row, 41
    Burns
    Carrity
    Flarety
    Learys
    McGraths
    O'Briens

Index

Ryans
Toohills
Irish Row Shamrocks, 41
Ives, Liver, 243
Ives, Paul, 41
Jones, Sam, 122
K-Theater (Clinton, Illinois), 52
Karr, Hunger, 30, 31
Karr, Mousie, 25, 29, 30, 33, 34, 40, 42, 44
Karr, Mulligan, 36
Kinders, 18, 44, 60
Kinder, Harry, 18
Kinder, Spud, 60, 243, 251
Kinder, Virgil, 251
King, Bill, 222
King, Dick, 66
Lash, Walter, 171
Lay, Marvin, 169
Lay, Walter, 169, 171
Leasure, E.E., 131, 132
Lehman Dairy, 50
Lillard, Mrs., 72
Lincoln, Abraham, 12, 26
Longbrakes, 9, 16, 19, 37, 79
Longbrake, (Julius) Chink, 25, 31, 33, 40, 42, 57, 58
Longbrake, June, 30
Lovellette, Clyde, 10
MacAninch, Bob, 135
Maurer, Harold, 149
Maurer, Ruth, 149

Index

McCannon, Dale, 76, Family Tree
McCannon, Dean, 49, 74-76, 78, 140, Family Tree
McCannon, Fred, 49, Family Tree
McCannon, Ines, Family Tree
McCannon, Olive Gardner, 114, 116, 119, 121, 125, 127, 130, 132, 1?
    137, 138, 151, 189, 234, Family Tree
McCastle, Static, 60
McDermott, Mr., 72
McKay, Jack, 222
Melton, Monroe, 77
Miller Park Zoo, 248, 251
Moberlys, 17, 19, 43
Moberly, Bert, 79
Moberly, Billy, 36, 40, 44
Mohr, Glen, 222, 253
Mooreville School (DeWitt Country, Illinois), 16, 19, 21, 26, 31, 43
Nash Car Club of America, 265
O'Brien, Paul, 219
Palmer, Old Man, 88
Pate, Willie, 231
Peterson, Carolyn McCannon, 127, 150, 219, Family Tree
Peterson, Charles, 10, 265
Peterson, Michael, 243, 265, Endorsements, Family Tree
Peterson, Ted, 265, Endorsements, Family Tree
Phillips Boys, 67
Phillips, Earl, 65, 66
Poston, Louie, 67
Powell, Porter, 76
Powers, Paul, 245
Prairie Center, Illinois, 52

Index

Prince, Bob, 62, 64, 67
Progress School Bearcats, 43
Pryor, Richard, 234
Reiter, Bill, 83, 132
Ramseyer, Judge, 252
Reynolds, Buck, 31
Rhodes, Dusty, 87
Riley, Deane, 143, 144
Rinkydinks, 42
Rogers, Lou, 222
Rolofson, Frank, 81, 253
Rolofson, Hugh, 116
Rolofson, Loren, 81, 252
Rolofson, Louie, 43, 252
Rolofson, Minnie, 9, 81, Family Tree
Rolofson, Monte, 55, 81, 253
Rolofson, Roy, 11, 18, 40, 42-44, 54-56, 59, 81, 82, 244, 252
Rolofson, Twila, 59
Ross, Arby, 59
Ross, Geraldine, 59
Roundfield, Carroll, 233, 234
Rutledge, Ann, 12
Salt Creek Timber Wolves, 43
Schmidt, Pete, 222
Schneider, Joe, 230
Seltzer, Bernie, 225
Shaw, Paul, 105, 106
Shearer, Al, 61
Shere, Watsie, 202
Sheriff King, 236

Index

Shockey, Harry, 217, 222
Shockey, Marie, 225
Short, Henry, 82
Slagell, Burdell, 144
Smith, Les, 208
Smithson, Buzzy, 150
Snoddy, Jack, 64
Stagner, Curley, 64, 67
Stanton, Florence, 100, 101
Stanton, George, 13, 91, 99, 113
Stephens, Cy, 62
Stevens, Warren, 43
Stevenson, Adlai, 217
Stoltz, Jack, 67
Stone, Jack, 10
Streckfuss, Dick, 151
Suddith Road (Normal, Illinois), 73
Sullivan, Bill, 222
Sutter, Minnie McCannon, 9, Family Tree
Taylor, Archie, 43
Thomas, Buzz, 233
Thompson, Chester, 134
Thorpes, 11
Thorpe, Nelson, 51
Thorpe, Thornton, 152
Trent, (Eldon) Pete, 250
Trent, Mary Norma Sutter, 250
Turner, Spencer, 12, 13

Index

Veterinarians
    Dr. Bane, 154
    Dr. Clarno, 227
    Dr. Frank, 137, 153
    Dr. George, 146
    Dr. Gill, 138, 153
    Dr. Hayer, 205
    Dr. Hill, 138
    Dr. Little, 154, 227
    Dr. Lundquist, 113
    Dr. McLeod, 138
    Dr. Mosier, 138
    Dr. Oberst, 136
    Dr. Wainscott, 220
Wade, (Lawrence)Larry, 60, 77, 246
Wapella, Illinois, 13, 14, 43, 44, 59-61, 77-78, 152, 215, 243-244, 252
Warber, Eileen, 191
Wheatley, Hattie McCannon, 130
Whitneys, 81, 82
Whitney, Bill and Grace, 252, 253
Wilson, Andy, 54, 82
Wilson, (Willard) Willie, 9, 25, 31, 33, 34, 40, 44, 57

Acknowledgements

My special thanks go to my husband Charles Peterson who edited and encouraged. He also was my computer expert and financier. My sons Ted and Michael also were quick to find my typing and spelling errors and of course their enjoyment of rereading the stories helped keep me going. Any errors of spelling and grammar are solely my responsibility. I am convinced that there will be at least two more generations writing their adventures for the family's entertainment.

We have always joked that if we were lucky enough to increase our family by marriage or love, we would have to provide a special dictionary of Peterson references. These stories of my dad are a good start in understanding our family.

Thanks also to Jim Bracewell and Jack Frank who helped me with research on the 1928 Nash two-seater. When I called Cassoday, Kansas for permission to use a picture on the web, I found the willing and helpful owner of the Cassoday Café. Amy Campbell at the Bloomington, Illinois Public Library also quickly responded to my request for the newspaper articles on my dad.

The greatest thanks go to my dad who took the time and effort to write all these stories. I didn't realize until I started retyping the stories how much work he had done. But that is typical. Dad has always worked hard but made time to share with his family. Growing up I could

Acknowledgements

wander over to his office at ten o'clock at night when he had been up and working since five in the morning, and he always had time to laugh and talk.

Carolyn McCannon Peterson

Printed in the United States
39124LVS00002B/71